THE GREAT ALCHEMICAL WORK

BK 10⁰

RUBELLUS PETRINUS

The Great Alchemical Work
of Eirenaeus Philalethes, Nicholas Flamel and Basil Valentine

Translated from the Portuguese, and with Prefaces by,
Frater Parush and Rubaphilos

Edited by Paul Hardacre

SALAMANDER
AND SONS

Modern Magistery
an imprint of Salamander and Sons
Brisbane   Chiang Mai

First English edition published 2007 by
Salamander and Sons

P O Box 215
Prasing Post
Muang, Chiang Mai
Thailand 50205

www.salamanderandsons.com

For further information about Salamander and Sons titles please visit our website or write to the above address.

Edited by Paul Hardacre (www.paulhardacre.com)
Translated from the Portuguese, and with Prefaces by, Frater Parush and Rubaphilos
Cover design by Marissa Newell (www.marissanewell.com)
Printed in New Zealand by Astra Print
Typeset by Salamander and Sons in Leitura

National Library of Australia
Cataloguing-in-publication data

Petrinus, Rubellus.
[Grande obra alqui´mica de Ireneu Filaleto, Nicolau Flamel e Basilio Valentim. English]

The great alchemical work of Eirenaeus Philalethes, Nicholas Flamel and Basil Valentine.

English ed.
Bibliography.
ISBN 9780980409901 (pbk.).

1. Basilius Valentinus - Criticism and interpretation. 2. Philalethes, Eirenaeus - Criticism and interpretation. 3. Flamel, Nicolas, d. 1418 - Criticism and interpretation. 4. Alchemy. I. Parush, Frater. II. Rubaphilos. III.

Hardacre, Paul. IV. Title.

540.112

SOLVE

ET

COAGULA

FOR ALL BROTHERS IN ART

ACKNOWLEDGEMENTS

The author would like to thank Frater Parush for his welcome efforts in preparing the English translation of this little work.

The editor would like to thank Rubaphilos for his generous assistance in the form of numerous textual revisions and operative clarifications. Gratitude also to Dennis William Hauck and Duane Saari of the International Alchemy Guild, and Andrew Kettle of R.A.M.S. Digital, for their support and encouragement along the way. Special thanks to both Adam McLean and Ross Mack – the former, for his expertise regarding, and kind provision of, the 1602 rough woodcut versions of the first three of Basil Valentine's Twelve Keys; and the latter, for his patronage which enabled this little work to be shared with an English language readership.

CONTENTS

FIRST PREFACE

As part of my effort in preparing this work for an English language audience, Rubellus Petrinus has asked me to write a brief introduction. Rubellus is a Portuguese alchemist who, for all intents and purposes, has a well-defined knowledge of the classic tradition of our Art. His focus has been on that process which, within the alchemical circles I have frequented, alchemists commonly refer to as either the *Dry Way*, or as the *Flamel Work*.

There were two primary reasons why I chose to accept the invitation, by Rubellus, to help him with the preparation of this work. Firstly, because the author has an attitude about alchemy, as a discipline and a tradition, which I fully agree with and feel is important, today, to emphasise.

There is a trend that has developed in the last 200-300 years, and which has become increasingly more popular since the advent of Jungian psychology, towards insisting that alchemy is anything other than an operative laboratory Art. Some of these claims can, in the absolute broadest sense, be said to have some connection to alchemy as an *abstract concept*, but hardly as an age-old tradition. Many other such claims, though, have no link with traditional or abstract conceptual alchemy at all. One thing that all of these *alternative* definitions of 'alchemy' seem to share is that their adherents often have little or no idea about the operative tradition that *gave birth* to the discipline of alchemy and its classic literature.

The second reason for my interest in this present work is that, as a pilgrim on the path of the *Wet Way* myself, I had completed my initial apprenticeship in alchemy with no training in the *Dry Way*. Besides this I could find no literature in English that gave much more than a passing, *non-cryptic* mention of this very secret process. Therefore, I was very curious to look over this treatise with the hope of learning something – anything – about this interesting approach to the Great Work. I was, gladly, not disappointed at all.

With this in mind I consider this book immediately of great value to those with an *active* interest in alchemy. Not only is this publication the first of its kind, as far as I am aware, to explain so carefully, in the public arena, and so clearly, with little veiling and no deliberate misleading, the process of the Masters Flamel, Valentine and Philalethes; but it may also claim to be the first publication in modern times which deals so openly and directly with the Great Work; that is, with the *actual* preparation of the Philosopher's Stone, itself.

For this reason this work will not only be of great aid to novices who are looking ahead in contemplation of where their work may take them, but also to Adepts in the field who are looking to place once missing pieces of this puzzle into their proper places.

I should also point out here, for those who have travelled the *Wet Way*, that Rubellus has included information, indirectly, in this work, which throws light on aspects of the Wet Path as well.

One of my initial concerns, when asked to help prepare the English translation of this book, was that, because my knowledge of the Great Work almost exclusively resides in the area of the Wet Method alone, that I would have some difficulty in grasping the descriptions of substances and processes which make up the *Dry Way*. Those who, like myself, were not overly familiar with the Dry Path, either practically or theoretically, but who have general experience in the realm of mineral spagyrics, will be happy to know that Rubellus has presented his description of the *Dry Way* in such a manner that it is not outside the reaches of the experienced mineral alchemist who works in the traditional way. This, alone, I found a refreshing experience.

In addition to Rubellus' obvious knowledge of the practical application of alchemy, the interested student will find herein one of the best publications now available of the accurate and proper understanding of some important pieces of classic alchemical cypher. As anyone who has read classic alchemical literature will know all too well, its authors, in past ages, published their knowledge in both graphic and textual forms that were highly cryptic in nature; doing more to conceal information and confuse the uninitiated than to aid in any way at all. Rubellus, though, removes a good portion of the veil from over the works of Flamel, Valentine and Philalethes concerning the Great Work, and thereby opens the door to a wider understanding of other related literature.

Some modern authors, amongst them individuals claiming to be well educated in the esoteric arts, have taken advantage of what they believe is a complete ignorance in modern times concerning knowledge of the original meaning of these secretive teachings. Seeking to exploit this situation, they have encouraged their readers and followers to believe all manner of wild theories concerning our Art and its tradition. Rubellus has done us a great service, then, by helping to demystify this classical literature and thereby debunk those who would deliberately, or otherwise, lead others astray, by demonstrating that there is indeed still alive a circle of initiates who have preserved a pure understanding of the original meaning of these important works.

Rubellus closes his book with a few examples of very important spagyric processes that are indirectly related to the main subject of this work. The volatilisation of tartar and the preparation of Oil of Gold, for example, described in detail here, have been, by expert alchemists of all ages, considered key processes of great importance. These operations serve also as perfect examples of some of the problems in chemistry that conventional science has not grasped as yet, but which have been known of by experienced alchemists for long ages.

A final note on my effort to translate this English edition of Rubellus' work. My task involved cleaning up a rough machine translation from the original Portuguese into English, in order to

produce this edition in good English. Rubellus has used many
classical terms and phrases in his description of equipment and
the various operations involved. In the case of naming equipment
in most cases I have chosen to adhere to the classical terms used,
as I understand this to be one of the author's intentions, in an
effort to encourage the novice to investigate the Art further, and
thereby gain a better understanding of this material.

There were one or two other terms which were used by Rubellus
that I understood to be based on cultural linguistic oddities, which
I have taken the liberty to change into forms that would be better
understood by mainstream English speaking students, such as,
for example, the alteration of the term 'kaput' to 'caput mortem.'
Overall, though, the text is simplistic and straightforward and did
not present more than one or two minor problems in completing
the clean translation.

To sum up, then, in a short sentence, in my opinion, the benefit
this work can provide, I simply say this:

In the realm of traditional operative alchemy there is only one
kind of authority who stands within the circle of Light that *the*
Tradition sheds, that Brother who has practical knowledge of the
subject at hand and can speak from experience.

Frater Parush (A.H.S.)
The Old Ahuriri Spit, Napier, New Zealand
December 1999

SECOND PREFACE

It is with much pleasure that I find myself asked to append a second introduction to this work, after some eight years that it has taken to find a home for it in English publication. A great many changes have happened in the alchemical community in that space of time, with us having seen an increased influx of new souls attracted to the Work, wide-eyed and ready to learn. Unfortunately, though, with the increase in numbers of interested students in the Art we have also witnessed an increase in confusion concerning the simple basics of understanding Hermetic, alchemical philosophy. The source of this confusion, it seems, are the many new ideas of questionable value that have been introduced into the canon of alchemical knowledge, over the last decade, making what is already a difficult subject to study, even more problematic to the new student.

Under such conditions the written works, and teachings, of individuals such as Brother Rubellus Petrinus have gained greater value in the eyes of those who struggle in their search for accurate knowledge. A knowledge that has had *all that is superficial removed from it*, as the old Masters were apt to say; exposing for us the simple basic facts of that which we refer to as the *Great Work*.

After twenty years of studying, researching and teaching alchemy, both the inner (psycho-spiritual) and outer (laboratory) traditions, I am glad to say that I have been fortunate in finding myself in the company of a good number of serious, discriminating and intelligent Sons of the Art. Such individuals, I am confident, will receive Rubellus' little work with welcome, and recognise in its content a gift from one of the more pure streams of alchemical teaching, which is so important to the European school of thought.

At the dawn of an era when modern science is beginning to awaken to an understanding and acceptance of the kinds of truths the old Masters of esoteric lore once taught, we persevere in the hope that more volumes in the genre of this work will flow from the pens and keyboards of aspiring alchemical researchers, to help push back the barriers of misinformation that have clouded our eyes from the truth for so long.

Let us hope that we can cast a light upon the fact that our Art is also a science, and that its terminology, teaching, study, and practice should always be treated with scientific methodology. A methodology devoid of the hearsay, fashionable clichés, politics, and superstition that have marred alchemical teachings for more than 3,000 years.

Rubaphilos (A.H.S.)
Napier, New Zealand
July 2007

THE GREAT ALCHEMICAL WORK OF

Eirenaeus Philalethes and Nicholas Flamel

THE FIRST WORK

Alchemy has always held a very special fascination for people. At present, a new generation shows great curiosity and interest for this almost forgotten 'science.'

There have always existed individuals who desire to penetrate the legendary and the strange, and who venture to cross the entrance to the labyrinth that is alchemy.

Its followers usually work in silence, in a retreat in their houses, where they have installed a small laboratory. Their instruments are copies of those that their ancestors used, although adapted to modern conditions.

They don't seek the impossible, as is commonly said, but simply confirmation of that which is described in the old treatises that the Masters have left us, with a view to the obtaining of the *Universal Medicine*, also known as the Philosopher's Stone.

Today, alchemy cohabits peacefully with science, and it is not rare to see learned individuals in the various branches of science, medicine and letters, who practice the Real Art.

There has been much writing about the alchemical symbolism found in cathedrals, palaces and even the houses of the aristocracy. It is a fascinating work to try to unmask the secrets contained in those figures sculpted in stone by our ancestor Artists as testimony of their involvement in Hermes' 'science.'

In the symbolism of alchemy, so far as we know, fixed rules don't exist. Everything was, and still is, left to the author's imagination and creativity. This often gives motive to 'philosophical' speculations that, in general, have nothing to do with the reality of alchemy.

We have said that, in alchemy, there are no fixed rules in its symbolism. However, with respect to descriptive and practical alchemy, the old Masters used, frequently, a figurative language, almost always based on the Indo-European mythology, capable of being interpreted by one who has the necessary knowledge and verifies the results obtained in the operations they describe. Thus, it can be concluded with some certainty which chemical substances, metals or minerals, enter in to those operations and the *modus operandi*.

To illustrate this conclusion, we will analyse syntactically that which Philalethes, author of *Speculum veritatis*, wanted to transmit to us, allegorically, in the *first illustration* of this treatise.

First illustration from the *Speculum veritatis* series.

On the left side of the illustration we see a *wolf* eating a *young warrior*, who has dropped to the earth, with armor and helmet, holding a sword in his right hand. We also see a tree covered with foliage. In the centre, another warrior, on foot, older and bearded, with a crippled leg, armor and helmet, holds in his right hand a

18

blazing object that symbolises a fiery power and, in the left hand, a *cruciferous globe* with a *star* in the centre.

Above this globe, among the clouds, a *sheep* has a *star* marking on its shoulder, aimed at the globe. On the right side, there are two old men (alchemists), one of them receiving in his hands the *cruciferous globe* from the warrior. The other old man is attentively observing.

The symbolism is clear. The sagacious investigator and expert can easily verify that this is an allegorical representation of Philalethes' *First Work*, the *Dry Way* – that is to say, the *separation* and *purifications* – with a view to the obtaining of the *Starry Martial Regulus*, as we will see later. But, so that there is not any doubt, we will now explain this matter in more detail.

The wolf represents, allegorically, the mineral *subject* also known as the *Black Dragon*, Saturn's son, or royal '*Saturnie.*' Basil Valentine, in the First Key of his book, *Twelve Keys*, refers to his grizzly *Hungry Wolf* that eats every metal. Christophle Glaser also mentions it in his *Traité De La Chymie*. The warrior, that the wolf is to devour with the help *of Vulcan*, God of Fire (here represented by the older crippled warrior), symbolises *Mars*.

The cruciferous globe that Vulcan holds in his left hand and is giving to one of the old alchemists, is the symbol of the earth, or of the mineral subject, which the Artist has to seek and to identify to begin the work. The star that we see in the centre of the globe symbolises the *Starry Martial Regulus*, proceeding from the *separation* and succeeding *purifications*, carried out by the fire for the Salt. Under the cruciferous globe a stream runs, which symbolises *Our Living Water*, that is to say the *Mercury*, which will be *animated* later.

The sheep or Aries symbolises, astrologically, the favorable season for the beginning of the work, also clearly identified by the foliage of the tree. Besides, the metallic correspondence of Aries is the same as it is for Mars, the same generator of the starry sign of the *Martial Regulus* that attests to this canonical operation.

The old alchemists utilised the fact that the astrological signs and the planets have correspondences with certain metals. Besides this, a profusion of spagyrical symbols exists, not always in agreement, which makes the task of the investigator of Hermes' Art more difficult.

Over the centuries, thousands of alchemical books have been published. Many of them are considered principal works, and are still well known. They were written by great Masters: Geber, Raymond Lull, Albert the Great, Arnold Vilanueve, Basil Valentine, Cosmopolitan, Bernard Trevisan, Nicholas Flamel, Eirenaeus Philalethes, Kamala Jnana, and others.

At present, many alchemical books exist on the market. Everything is published regardless of quality, which, it can be said, can only be evaluated by one who knows the Art, and not by any editor. Thus, the less illustrious readers have been confronted with the most absurd texts, without any merit from the operative alchemical point of view. Unhappily, this is verified even at the international level, because it seems to be in fashion to publish everything that seems to link with alchemy, except facsimiles of original works, which are expensive.

Happily, for those that know how to separate the wheat from the chaff, works of the great Masters still exist on the international market, mainly in France, where they can be found in facsimile. Also, in the National Library of Lisbon, in Ajuda and in Mafra, one can find genuine treatises of classic alchemy, unhappily only accessible to those that know Latin.

Of the aforementioned authors' treatises, many of them are so hard to comprehend that he who dares to interpret them cannot be sure of arriving at a good understanding. Only an Adept that has accomplished the whole Path can truly understand.

Here, it will be pertinent for the reader to interrogate contemporary alchemists who claim to have accomplished the *Great Work*; that is, if such Adepts exist.

As far as we know, there exists a great Master in France at least, whom we knew personally. He was a man with a superior academic upbringing that peacefully cohabits with traditional alchemy and who, as far as we know, has already accomplished the alchemical Paths: *Wet, Dry* and *Brief.*

What do the alchemists really seek (with all those works and experiences patiently repeated, some of which are not exempt of risks) in their laboratories?

We have already explained this. They look for confirmation of that which is written in the books of our Art, with a view to the elaboration of the *Universal Medicine* or *Philosophical Stone.*

Many will think, and they will even say, that it is a pure waste of time, because we seek the impossible. For several reasons, we aren't of the same opinion. One of them is that the Masters have written thousands of alchemical books down through the centuries. What reason would the Masters have for writing those books if they had no foundation?

It is correct that many alchemical books were written in obscure language, for none but those who are experts in the Art could understand them.

Almost all of the alchemists of the classic age, when they wrote their first books, jealously guarded alchemy's secrets and always referred to them in a veiled way. In this way, they could not perpetuate the Art, nor give testimony of it, to a neophyte. Later books were usually written in less philosophical and more accessible language, some almost in clear language.

We could give you some examples, but we have limited ourselves just to the Masters whose works we are to comment upon in the first part of this volume: Eirenaeus Philalethes and Nicholas Flamel in the introduction of the *An Open Entrance to the Closed Palace of the King* and the *Testament*, respectively.

> Eirenaeus Philalethes: "I, being an anonymous adept, a lover of learning, and a philosopher, have decreed to write this little treatise of medicinal, and physical arcana, in the year 1645, after the Birth of Christ, and in the 23rd year of my age, to assist in conducting my straying brethren out of

the labyrinth of error, and with the further object of making my self known to other Sages, holding aloft a torch which may be visible far and wide to those who are groping in the darkness of ignorance ... I have written more plainly about this Art than any my predecessors; sometimes I have found myself on the very verge of breaking my vow, and once or twice had to lay down my pen for a season; but I could not resist the inward prompting of God, which impelled me to preserve in most loving course, who alone knows the heart, and to whom only be glory for ever."

Nicholas Flamel: "I Nicholas Flamel, a scrivener of Paris, in the year 1414, in the reign of our gracious Prince Charles the VI, whom God preserve; and after the death of my faithful partner Perrenelle, am seized with a desire and a delight, in remembrance of her, and in your behalf, dear nephew, to write out the whole magistery of the secret of the Powder of Projection, or the Philosophical Tincture, which God had willed to impart to his very insignificant servant, and which I have found out, as thou also will find out in working as I shall declare unto you.

And for this cause do not forget to pray to God to bestow on thee the understanding of the reason of truth of nature, which thou wilt see in this book, wherein I have written the secrets word for word, sheet by sheet, and also as I have done and wrought with they dear aunt Perrenelle, whom I very much regret."

It is evident that the texts are not as clear as its authors say they are. Therefore, the Masters affirm, and with just reason, that it is not possible to achieve the Great Work only through literary study. If it wasn't for the charity of a Master or a Brother of the Art who provides help, we couldn't reach that knowledge completely, because in each Path there exists an unsurpassable obstacle. We know that well, even from our own experience.

In those times the old alchemists faced great dangers if they were discovered, as Philalethes tells us in his book, *An Open Entrance to the Closed Palace of the King*:

> "Yet we are not the murderers of our brethren; we are anxious only to do good to our fellow-men. But even our kindness and charitable compassion is rewarded with black ingratitude – ingratitude that cries to heaven for vengeance. It was only a short time ago, after visiting the plague-stricken haunts of a certain city, and restoring the sick to perfect health by means of miraculous medicine, I found myself surrounded by a yelling mob, who demanded that I should give to them my Elixir of the Sages; and it was only by changing my dress and my name, by shaving off my beard and putting on a wig, that I was enabled to save my life, and escape from hands of those wicked men ..."

> "Again, if you desire to sell any large quantity of your gold and silver, you will be unable to do so without imminent risk of discovery. The very fact that anyone has a great mass of bullion for sale would in most places excite suspicion. This feeling will be strengthened when people test the quality of our gold; for it is much finer and purer than any gold which brought from Barbary, or from the Guinea Coast; and our silver is better even than which is conveyed home by the Spanish silver fleet. If, in order to baffle discovery, you mix these precious metals with alloy, you render yourself liable, in England and Holland at least, to capital punishment; for in those countries no one is permitted to tamper

with the precious metals, except the officers of the
mint, and licensed goldsmiths."

We have thought that this was more than enough reason for
the alchemists to maintain their anonymity and the keeping of
their secrets. However, to uphold the Tradition and to assure that
its knowledge wasn't lost and, at the same time, to safeguard their
existence, they recorded their knowledge in the books that we
know of today, mostly writing under a nom de plume.

Today, as in the past, alchemists exist that are self-proclaimed
Adepts claiming to have accomplished the Great Work. Unhappily,
the works that they have produced have nothing to do with
traditional alchemy. Even so, they attract the curious and the
incautious and, ironically, even the experts that follow these
instructions until the bubble is burst.

Some of those alchemists obtain, as final product of such
works, a type of 'medicine' which they call 'universal,' but it has
not any medicinal virtue.

As the graphic and textual description of several alchemical
works is rendered to philosophical speculation, usually they are
accepted as being accurate by those that don't know the Art. Such
alchemists are so convinced of the validity of their works that
they often affirm that their processes have many a coincidence
parallel with some traditional methods, namely, with the work
of Eirenaeus Philalethes, or that the way of this great Master is the
Red Dragon Path.

The reader, certainly, will find this symbolic language strange.
In alchemy this is how it is, it always was and it will continue to
be, in respect for the Tradition. The alchemists write for those that
already have some knowledge of the Art.

We hope here to satisfy the reader's legitimate curiosity, he who
has a certain interest in the Art of Hermes – otherwise it would be
a waste of his time in reading this book. We can say that the *Red
Dragon* is the symbolic name of a mineral whose characteristics
correspond to the mythological dragon – an animal that kills,

NICOLAVS FLAMELLVS

Portrait of Nicholas Flamel.

with its hot and poisonous breath, all that it breathes upon. And, in fact, the dangers are like this in some phases of the Work. The same happens to be the case with the *Black Dragon*.

We have referred to the Philalethes Path, and we have done this intentionally, because it is the work of both Philalethes and Flamel that we will comment upon in the first part of this book, in order to demonstrate to the skeptics and detractors of the Art that alchemical texts describe accurately, not only the materials' real names, but also the *modus operandi* and the results achieved, so they may be properly interpreted.

We desire, also, to demonstrate to certain pseudo-alchemists and, above all, to some intellectuals that practice living-room alchemy, that their beautiful philosophical alchemical speeches, in practice, don't serve much for anything.

Eirenaeus Philalethes is one of the most controversial alchemists. His must famous work is *An Open Entrance to the Closed Palace of King*. This work has always been very much appreciated by all students of the Art. The great Sir Isaac Newton studied it deeply and, according to Betty Dobbs' book, *Les Fondements de l'Alchimie de Newton*, this scientist carried many experiences with a view to the accomplishment of the Philalethes Work. It appears that Newton never was able to conclude it though. He took the same way that we have ourselves already and, probably, he found the same difficulties that are still struggled with today by all those that look into the Philalethes Work: the *animation of Mercury*.

At the proper time, we will point out the obstacle that, for more than twenty years, has impeded us in the understanding of the Work, even though it is a simple matter.

Besides Philalethes' *An Open Entrance to the Closed Palace of the King*, he wrote other important works, including *The Marrow of Alchemy*. Some people also attribute the *Speculum veritatis* to him.

Nicholas Flamel, one of the most well known classic alchemists, wrote several works, the most important being *His Exposition of the Hieroglyphicall Figures*, *The Summary of Philosophy*,

The Wanted Desire and *Testament*. This last one, as we have already seen, is dedicated to his wife Perenelle's nephew. The original *Testament*, it seems, was hand-written in the margin of the pages of a vellum Psalm book, in Nicholas Flamel's own handwriting, for his nephew. Later, it was discovered, deciphered and copied by Master Dom Pernety.

In this book, Flamel describes an alchemical path that is very similar to that of Philalethes, but differing in some operative details. We would suggest reading these works completely, because what is omitted in one is almost revealed in detail in the other. It is through these two works that we will be aided in describing and commenting upon the *Amalgam Path*.

As we have already said, it is more than twenty years since we sought in vain the exit from the labyrinth that leads to the *Second Work* of this particular path. Thanks to Flamel's *Testament*, we were able to go on to the second step of the Work, because with the first step much time had passed before we could complete it.

We give thanks to the Lady and also to the Masters that, with their charitable teachings, helped us to enter in through the second door of the Sanctuary. God willing, you, sons of the Art that read us, can also accomplish this with the help of our humble work.

By these means we know the Philalethes Path and Flamel's are essentially composed of two different phases. This means that the first operations should be executed in the oven, in a ceramic refractory crucible, with temperatures of about one thousand degrees. The second phase will be made at the lowest temperature, in a sandstone or stainless steel retort, and with a Pyrex glass matrass, in an oven called an *athanor*.

We know that there will be those who don't agree with us but, to these, we invite you to prove your opposition with valid arguments. Given this, let us see, then, what Philalethes says regarding the first phase of his work in *The Marrow of Alchemy* and in *An Open Entrance to the Closed Palace of King*:

"The substance which we first take in hand is a mineral similar to Mercury, which a crude sulphur doth bake in the Earth; it is called Saturn's Child, which indeed appeareth vile to sight, but is glorious within; it is sable coloured, with argent veins appearing intermixed in the body, whose sparkling line stains the connate sulphur; it is wholly volatile and unfixed, yet taken in its native crudity, it purgeth all superfluity of Sol; it is of a venomous nature, and abused by many in a medicinal way; if its elements by Art be loosed, the inside appears very resplendent, which then floweth in the fire like a metal, although there is nothing of a metallic kind more brittle."

Philalethes describes with great exactitude and detail our mineral subject's main characteristics, with a view to its identification for the children of the Art. Flamel is less generous and, until the *separation*, veils completely the subject's name and its metallic acolyte. Philalethes begins by saying that the mineral subject of his work is Saturn's son. As it is known, astrologically, Saturn is a dark and cold planet, and its metallic correspondence is lead, whose mineral, a black metallic colour, is galena.

Our mineral, being Saturn's son, has very similar characteristics to its mineral progenitor. It is sable coloured (sable, in heraldry, corresponds to black) with silver veins and its shine is stained by an innate sulphur. It is volatile, poisonous, it *purges* the Sun's superfluities and, at that time in history, it was used and abused by many doctors and chemists in the practice of the medicine. He says, still, that its inner is bright, that it flows in fire, and as a metal that in its solid state is very brittle.

Well then, what can we deduce from that which we have said about the mineral subject?

That it is a black mineral, brilliant in colour, whose shine is stained by innate chemical sulphur. For now, we can conclude that these characteristics correspond, exactly, to one sulfide mineral ore. That it *purges* the Sun (gold) of its superfluity. Anciently, to *purge* (to purify) gold, besides the quartation process (cementing and amalgamating with common quicksilver), our Artists melted impure gold with our mineral, which, after volatilisation with a strong fire (our mineral is volatile), left the gold in the crucible bottom, exempt of impurities.

In effect, and with great incidence in the 17th-19th centuries, there were many cases of poisoning form the indiscriminate abuse of this mineral as a medicine, mainly as a purgative; not only the raw mineral, but also its regulus, being prescribed.

It flows in the fire as a metal, is very brittle in its solid state and can easily be powdered in a metal mortar (see Plate I-a). Indeed this mineral is described well. We shall include a little extra fact, that the planetary symbol of this mineral is the same as that used for the Earth, that is to say a cruciferous globe.

We cannot add anything else, because everything has already been said. There is not a word or a superfluous point that is lacking, as Philalethes affirms in his book.

It is almost impossible, for those who have some mineralogical and metallurgical knowledge, not to know what mineral is here described.

This mineral subject has been formerly found in abundance in our country.[1] At present, some mines from which it was extracted are no longer in activity or are obstructed; therefore, it is no longer easy to find it here.

Saying this, we can continue looking at the description of the first part of the *First Work*, because the mineral subject doesn't have all the necessary elements to complete the process.

> "But it contained in itself no Sulphur, save only it is congealed by a burning sulphur, being brittle, and black with shining veins."

---

1 This of course refers to the author's country of residence, Portugal.

"They sought active sulphur in a pure state, and found it cunningly concealed in the House of the Ram."

"It seemed strange indeed, that a metal so stout and fixed as to withstand the thundering blast of Vulcan, which will not relent in any heat, nor mix in flux with any metal, yet by our Art, it will in this piercing mineral liquor be made retrograde."

"Moreover Aries is known to the house of stout Mars, in which all artists charge you to begin in your work, and what can be said more plainly? Surely there can be none so ignorant as not to believe that a hidden meaning is concealed in these words, which hitherto was never better explained."

Before we continue we will have to explain what the Master wants to say in the use of the term *Sulphur* (alchemical). The basis of Hermetic theory is matter's unity. It is a unity but it can take several forms and, in these new forms, combine and produce new bodies. Matter is composed of two principles: *Sulphur* and *Mercury*, which can be combined in different proportions to form new bodies.

Basil Valentine adds a third principle: *Salt*. The terms Sulphur, Mercury and Salt don't refer to the chemical bodies that are known commonly by these names, but instead describe certain qualities of matter. The Sulphur, in a metal, refers to its colour and to its degree of combustibility; Mercury, to its shine, volatility, fusibility, and malleability; Salt, to the product of a union between Sulphur and Mercury, according to some people, and its hardness, according to others.

Given these explanations, indispensable for the understanding of the text, we can continue.

Philalethes says that the mineral subject doesn't contain any Sulphur, but that only chemical sulphur coagulates it. As we saw, this is true, for it is a sulphide mineral ore. He tells us still, to seek that Sulphur we require in the house of Aries or Mars, which both mean the same thing, in a metal whose zodiacal correspondence is that of Aries or the Ram and, the planetary, of Mars. It is impossible to be clearer, because it isn't difficult to know which is the metal corresponding to the Martian planet, whose spagyric symbol is the same that universally designates the masculine sex.

The Master adds, and with much pertinence, that it is strange to see a metal so stout (not volatile) be retrograded (to return to the sulphide state) through the Art, by the penetrating power of our mineral. Philalethes, as great a Master that he was in our Art, for his time showed to have a great metallurgical and spagyrical knowledge, which causes us to think that he must have been a great and learned man.

At present, we know that this metal (Mars) once melted with our subject, takes possession of its Sulphur, reducing the mineral sulphide to a metal (regulus), it being then combined with the chemical sulphur in the sulphide form (caput), which is one of the original ways that the ore of metallic Mars was usually extracted.

Of this, therefore, the Master tells us that this penetrating mineral has the power to retrograde Mars; that is, to transform it again (artificially) into a sulphide of Mars.

In the following, Philalethes tells us those proportions that it is necessary to respect in order to proceed to the *separation*, that is, toward the obtaining of a Martial Regulus, and of the respective caput.

> "Let me tell you now how this part of work is performed. Take 4 parts of our fiery Dragon, in whose belly is hidden the magic Chalybs, and 9 parts of our Magnet; mingle them by means of a fierce fire, in the form of a mineral water, the foam of which must be taken away. Remove the shell, and take the kernel. Purge what remains once more by means of fire and the Sun, which may be done easily if Saturn shall have seen himself in the mirror

of Mars. Then you will obtain our Chameleon, or Chaos, in which all the virtues of our Art are potentially present."

"First then cause Mars to embrace this mineral, so shall both cast away their earthiness, and in short space the metalline substance shall shine like the heavens and for a sign of your success, you shall surely find a seal of a stellate kind imprinted thereon."

"... dregs being removed, there appears a nut in fashion like to a metal (which may be powdered to dust) wherein is shut, like a tender soul, which in a small fire arises as smoke, similar to Argent-vive, slightly congealed, which the fire does evaporate."

"This substance is of a stellate nature, and wholly spiritual, being totally inclined to fly from the fire; the reason is because the soul of each is a magnet to each other, and this we call the urine of old Saturn. This is our steel, our true hermaphrodite, our Moon, so named for its brightness ..."

"When you see its constellation, follow it to the cradle, and there you will behold a beautiful Infant. Remove the impurities, look upon the face of the King's Son; open your treasury, give to him gold, and after his death he will bestow on you his flesh and blood, the highest Medicine in the three monarchies of the earth."

The Master could not elucidate further. First, he gives us the proportions: four parts of the igneous Dragon for nine parts of our Magnet. But, pay attention, there is an ambush here. He says:

> "... Take four parts of the igneous Dragon that hides
> in its womb the magic steel (Sulphur) and nine
> parts of our Magnet ..."

We know that the mineral subject (our *Black Dragon*) is lacking actual alchemical Sulphur. Therefore, the carrier of Sulphur will be, as he affirms, Mars, so much more that in advance he says:

> "She attracts it (Sulphur) as a Magnet,"

which meaning designates our mineral as the Magnet.

> "Leaves the crust and it takes the nucleus, purges it
> three times for the fire and the Salt ..."

Although somewhat synthetically, Philalethes now teaches us how to make the *separation* and the *purification* with a view to the obtaining of the *Starry Martial Regulus*. First, by melting the subject with Mars, separating them; then he refers to the caput. Next follows the *purification* with two suitable salts until the *star* appears (see Plate I-b).

Philalethes and Flamel both omit an operation whose execution is indispensable before the *separation* is carried out: the *purge*. This operation allows us to *purge* (to purify) the mineral of the silica impurities that usually defile it.

The alchemical oven should already be built with view to this operation. For this, it is necessary to construct a hole in the bottom of the oven, over which is placed, afterwards, the crucible, which also has an 8 or 10 millimetre hole in its bottom.

In order to carry out the *purge*, put the mineral in small pieces into the crucible, until it is filled, and replace its lid.

Put the crucible in the oven, taking care of verifying that the hole in the bottom of the crucible coincides with the one in the oven. Underneath the oven bottom is placed a glass container filled with rainwater.

Light the gas torch and introduce it into the appropriate opening constructed in a suitable side of the oven. When the mineral reaches its melting point, it will drip through the holes of the crucible and the oven, dropping into the container filled with water, solidifying, as it does, into granules. A scum will stay in the crucible and it should be removed while it is still hot. Take care not to breathe in the poisonous *Black Dragon's* breath.

Flamel, in his *Testament*, is less greedy in the description of the *modus operandi* and also with the identification of the two acolytes that take part in the melting process. As for procedure, we will see how he explains it:

> "Take thou in the first place the eldest or first-born child of Saturn, not the vulgar, 9 parts; of the sabre chalibs of the God of War, 4 parts. Put this latter into a crucible, and when it comes to a melting redness, cast therein the 9 parts of Saturn, and immediately this will redden the other. Cleanse thou carefully the filth that arises the surface of saturnia, with saltpetre and tartar, four or five times. The operation will be rightly done when thou seest upon the matter an astral sign like as star."

Basically, this is an operation known to a good metallurgist that consists of melting, with an appropriate heat, the reduced *purged* mineral powdered with the metal in filings, in the suggested proportions. The melting process, as Flamel says, involves the use of two different salts as a flux: saltpeter and tartar, or the vegetable salt of wine. We will include that the required proportions of the two salts together are 1/15 of the total mass. The salts that compose the flux should be, as much as possible, of natural origin.

The nitre or saltpeter, a name composed of the words salt and lithos, meaning 'stone salt.'

Flowers (white powdery salts) of natural nitre can be found at several places on the earth's surface, dried by the action of the sun's rays. Often it appears covering the walls of certain natural grottos opened in the calcareous rocks, and can be found on the wet walls of buildings where animals are kept, such as in stables.

At present, you might find it will be almost impossible to get the *first salt* (nitre) from its natural environment.

There is, however, a way to prepare it, using the commercial salt revivified in the natural environment that it originates in. In this way it can be daily within your reach, and if there isn't another process that allows you to obtain natural nitre, we cannot overlook this way of preparing from commercial salt.

Obtain and store at least 10 litres of the organic urine of any ruminant animal, or from yourself. Putrefy it in large 5 litre plastic bottles and, only then, you can use it to revivify your commercial nitre.

Acquire a ceramic pot, not glazed, with a capacity of 10-15 litres. Place it, preferably, in a basement or attic, or in a place sheltered from solar light.

Pour in 10 litres of the organic urine, putrefied, and 4 kilograms of the commercial nitre. Mix well with a wooden stick, to dissolve the salt as best as possible. Place a ceramic cover on the mouth of your pot and a plastic plate underneath, to catch the liquid that will eventually leak out through the walls of the pot.

If you don't have a suitable place to put the pot, we advise you not to put it in your apartment or flat due to the bad smell that exhales from the contents of the pot.

After a few days the salt will begin to form, because of the porosity of the pot, on its outside wall in a form of a fluff (see Plate I-d). When you have enough, remove it with a paintbrush or with a wooden spatula. Next, dissolve it in hot rainwater, in a stainless steel container.

After all of the salt has been dissolved in this manner, filter the hot liquid and pour it into a large glass bottle, through a plastic or glass funnel, and using a cotton filter. Pour the filtered liquid into a stainless steel container and place it upon the fire again, to evaporate the excess water. Take care not to let the temperature rise over more than 60 degrees Celsius. When the water has reduced to a third of its original volume, remove the evaporating dish from the fire and place it in a location sheltered from the sunlight.

The following day, you will find that in the dish that the salt has crystallised into agglomerations of needles, as you can observe in the accompanying image (see Plate I-c).

With a spoon, remove the salt and dry it in a very clean white cotton cloth. If the salt is not white and crystalline, dissolve it again and crystallise it as previously. After drying, keep it in a tightly closed, large-mouthed glass flask sheltered from the light.

In relationship to the second salt, as we live in a country that produces wine, it will be easy for us to obtain it in a natural condition.

Tartar can be extracted from the dregs of the wine making process. The best tartar is deposited as large crystals on the bottom, or on the walls, of wine barrels. This salt is dissolved in boiling tap water to the proportion of 1/18.

Acquire, at least, 10 kilograms of wine tartar produced from white wine, as it is easier to purify it. Grind it into a rough powder in an iron mortar. In a stainless steel bowl heat up 10 litres of tap water until it boils. Pour in, little by little, 0.5 kilograms of powdered tartar. Leave it boiling for some time until all of the salt is well dissolved. While the water is still boiling, with an enameled mug or cup pour it into another similar bowl, through a very clean cotton cloth, to filter it.

Let it rest for twelve hours. The salt will crystallise into small crystals that you will remove and will place to dry in the sunlight, on a cotton cloth. Repeat the same operation with all of your tartar.

The salt of the first crystallisation will be very impure; therefore, you will have to repeat the process to obtain the whitest salt. Keep it in a well closed, large-mouthed glass jar.

The *separation* is made in the following manner: place a ceramic refractory crucible, with its cover, in a gas oven. First, put in the crucible our warrior reduced to filings, and replace the crucible cover. When it is reddened, pour, in successive phases, the powdered mixture of the mineral and the flux; mix with an iron rod. After everything is well liquefied, drain the melted metal into a stainless steel conic mould previously warmed and greased with oil or suet, and let it cool slowly. The caput will be on the surface and the regulus, because it is heavier, sinks to the bottom.

After it is well cooled, remove the regulus from the mould and, holding it in your hand with the help of a leather glove, separate the regulus form the caput mortem with a hammer blow applied to the caput mortem-regulus junction point.

Afterwards, in a metal mortar, grind the regulus roughly and then pour it into a crucible with its cover replaced and melt it using the flux again, in suitable proportions, in order to obtain the *Starry Martial Regulus*.

The geometric crystalline lines looking like a 'star,' that appear on its surface after taking it out the vitriolic crust, show the sign of the regulus' purity. It is this sign that the ancient alchemists named the *star*. Therefore, Philalethes says:

> "When you see its constellation (star), follow it to the cradle, and there you will behold a beautiful Infant (*Starry Martial Regulus*). Remove the impurities, look upon the face of the King's Son ..."

In fact, if the *separation* and the Mercurial *purifications* were properly executed, breaking the regulus obliquely, you will verify that its crystallisation was made in laminations like mica, and shining as if it was polished silver.

We should include here that in the properly performed *Dry Way's* First Work, there is a preliminary operation to execute usually not referred to: the *assation*.

This is what Philalethes describes in this part of the verses of *The Marrow of Alchemy* or in *An Open Entrance to the Closed Palace of the King*, as well as Flamel in his *Testament*.

It is evident that they fail to describe here some very important small operative details, but these, as tradition asserts, they would only teach mouth-to-ear, from a Master or a Brother of the Art. However, we think that the essentials have been said.

Finally, Philalethes writes:

> "... after his death he (the *Starry Martial Regulus*) will
> bestow upon you his flesh and blood, the highest
> Medicine in the three monarchies of the earth."

And, in fact, it is just like this. The *Starry Martial Regulus* is, without doubt, the base of departure for the whole Work. This matter will attain, as our final goal, the *Universal Medicine* or *Philosopher's Stone*.

After everything that we have said, demonstrated and confirmed unequivocally, will there still be anybody so skeptical as to doubt what our Masters have written concerning our Art?

With all the references that we have given you concerning the preparation of the salts, material proportions and *modus operandi*, we have been extremely charitable because we have told you in a few lines what we have taken years to discover and to learn with our Masters. Therefore, don't think that, from this point, it will be as easy as this; you will have to travel your own way.

Certainly, you will notice that we have referred to the materials' classic names, including the salts, just as they were known in earlier times, though we have remained silent, intentionally, on some details of its canonical preparation that, if only for the Art's sake, they remain a true Herculean work. This will, then, be your research job. In the enclosed bibliography, you will find the titles of the works where you can learn what it is necessary to know about the preparation of the salts we have referred to, and in this same manner, other suitable spagyric operations.

Don't forget that, in order for you to understand the materials terminology and the various kinds of laboratory equipment mentioned in the classic literature of alchemy, you would have to refer to the knowledge of that time in reference to the sciences and the arts. The practice of alchemy can't be faced only with a basis in the positivist knowledge of our times.

If you understand everything that we have told you, practically, in clear language, without sophism, lacking only in reference to the material's actual chemical designation, then you have ascended the *first step* of our Art. Even so, if you still didn't identify the mineral subject and its metallic acolyte, including the salts that compose the flux, then it is pertinent to refer here to the great Master Basil Valentine where, at the end of the First Key of his book *Twelve Keys*, he said:

> "If now you understand what I say, then have you opened the first lock with this KEY ... but if you cannot find any light herein, then will not your glass spectacles profit you anything, nor your natural eyes help you find out that at last which you would at the beginning."

Symbol of the *Starry Martial Regulus*.

THE SECOND WORK

The purpose of the *First Work*, as we saw, is the obtaining of the *Starry Martial Regulus*.

In the *Amalgam Path*, the regulus, of itself, is not enough to complete the Work; for being a dry and brittle body, without radical humidity, it needs, therefore, a liquid agent that it can incorporate.

This agent is the *water* that doesn't wet the hands. This water, according to the Masters, lacks alchemical *Sulphur*, for which reason it requires the addition of an element that has it already.

The *Starry Martial Regulus*, as we know, has in its womb the Sulphur that was introduced to it through the *separation*. Therefore, it is in a suitable condition for supplying to the water the Sulphur that is lacking and that received itself from Mars.

Thus, introducing by skill in the Art into this water a true Sulphur, it will become philosophical and capable of our Work. After this operation, which we will describe further, our water will become a hermaphrodite or androgynous, by incorporating into its body the Sulphur (male) and the Mercury (female).

After this small introduction, let us see what Philalethes says about this water that doesn't wet the hands, with view to its identification by the Art's sons:

> "Wherefore now observe, that our Son of Saturn, must be united to a metalline, and mercurial form, because it is Argent-Vive alone, which is the agent our work requires, but common argent-vive availed nothing to our Stone, being dead, yet it is inclined to be accuated by the salt of Nature, and true Sulphur, which is its only mate."

"And although some of the metals may be mixed
with Argent-vive, yet do they not enter each other
otherwise than as to sight, but by heat may easily
be driven from each other, for you will find that
they never penetrate the centre, nor will either of
them be altered for better."

"And there is only one body in the Earth, which
is so nearly allied to Mercury, as is fit to prepare it
for our secret stone, and to hide the solid body in
this womb, this as I said before is the off-spring of
Saturn. Well known to all the Magi, and which I
have shown."

Philalethes could not be clearer in the identification of *Our
Water* that thus releases us from any further comment.

The Master tells us that:

"And there is only one body in the Earth, which
is so nearly allied to Mercury, as is fit to prepare it
for our secret stone, and to hide the solid body in
this womb, this as I said before is the off-spring of
Saturn ..."

Thus, we know that common quicksilver will be allied with the
Starry Martial Regulus and receive from it the Sulphur introduced
to its womb.

Try, with suitable precaution (because quicksilver vapours are
extremely toxic) to amalgamate, in a Pyrex or porcelain mortar,
the *Starry Martial Regulus* thinly powdered in a metal mortar, with
common quicksilver. You will see that the quicksilver and the
regulus refuse to amalgamate, and neither will Vulcan's help aid
us, confirming that which Philalethes wisely tells us:

"...but strange it seemed to them, that as soon
and this Dragon came near the Spring the Waters,
as though afraid, did straightway retire, nor could
Vulcan's help at all avail, to reconcile them; then

appeared Diana's Doves in bright shining attire, with whose silver wings the air was calmed, wherein the infolded Dragon lost his sting ..."

"This thief is armed with all the malignity of arsenic, and is feared and eschewed by the winged youth. Though the Central Water be his Spouse, yet the youth cannot come to her, until Diana with the wings of her doves purges the poisonous air, and opens a passage to the bridal chamber. Then the youth enters easily through the pores, presently shaking the waters above, and stirring up a rude and ruddy cloud. Do thou, O Diana, bring in the water over him, even unto the brightness of the Moon! So the darkness on the face of the abyss will be dispersed by the spirit moving in the waters."

What is then necessary to allow the intimate union of the regulus and the quicksilver?

The Master tells us that it is accomplished by *Diana's Doves*. Here is one of the *Second Work* keys!

It is easy, even for one who has much experience and knowledge in the Art, to get lost at this crossroad.

"We have spoken out more plainly than any of our predecessors: and our Receipt, apart from the fact that we have not called things by their proper names, is perfectly trustworthy."

We will advise you that you may also need the help and charity of a Master or Brother in the Art. It is, in fact, that kind of help that we would give you here, but we lament that we cannot do so as clearly as we would like, because tradition imposes upon us certain limits. Besides, as we have already declared, you will have to travel your own way, as have we, and other Brothers already before you.

For Charities sake we will point out this problem so that it does not befall you, as it did us, to find yourself stalled for more that twenty years without leaving this crossroad.

Philalethes, in the works *An Open Entrance to the Closed Palace of the King* and in *The Marrow of Alchemy*, describes at least two different ways that allow the intimate union of the regulus with the quicksilver, which is the preparation of the *Philosophical Mercury* (see Plate I-e).

The first way, as we saw, is by means of Diana's Doves.

Unhappily, this way, the most difficult, isn't accessible to us because we are ignorant of just what exactly the two Doves of Diana are. The Master did not give us any clue that allows us to identify them.

We have been speculating very much concerning these two Doves, but until now, we still have not found any of Philalethes' works or those of any other alchemist that can give us a clue that allows us to find an exit from this problem. We once thought that they were two salts, probably silver chloride (horned Diana) or ammonium chloride, and the other salt as possibly potassium carbonate (salt of tartar), but we are not sure of this.

The Master, foreseeing exactly this difficulty, advises us to seek an alternative way:

> "Some in order to prepare their Water, use the Doves of Diana, which is a most tedious labour, that even for an artist to hit it once right, he may twice unfortunately miss: but the other way, (which is the most secret), we recommended to all that mean to be true artists."

In *The Marrow of Alchemy*, he makes reference to this secret way:

> "To this add Venus in a due proportion, whose beauty is admired by Mars, and she is known to have great love and desire to be joined unto him, when she to motion is soon inclined, as being allied

to gold, Mars, and bright Diana, with whom she conciliated love, and true union."

Flamel, being more charitable, describes this operation (the other, most secret way) more clearly, which helped us to better understand Philalethes' approach:

> "Then is made the key and the sabre, which opens and cuts through all metals, but chiefly Sun, Moon and Venus, which it eats, devours and keeps in his belly, and by this means thou art in the right road of truth, if thou has operated properly."

> "Marry thou therefore the young god Mercury, that is to say quicksilver with this which is the philosophic Mercury, that you may acuate by him and fortify the said running quicksilver, seven or even ten or eleven times with the said agent, which is called the key, or a steel sharpened sabre, for it cuts, scythes and penetrates all the bodies of the metals."

What may we conclude, here, about that which was said concerning this last method recommended by Philalethes, and also described by Flamel, although with some variants?

Philalethes nurtures, first, the *Starry Martial Regulus* with Diana or Venus and, only then, is it married with the quicksilver. Flamel first feeds the *Starry Martial Regulus* with the solar star or the lunar planet, then marries them, to proceed, with the young winged Mercury.

Here is the key that allowed us to open the door of the *Second Work* and that, now, we charitably reveal to you in plain language. Take to-the-letter everything that above we have told you and you will be gratified.

Let us see, now, what Philalethes says concerning the *modus operandi* and its purpose.

"But Mercury needs inward and essential purging, which radical cleansing is brought about by the addition of true Sulphur, little by little, according to the number of the Eagles."

"Thus, at the bidding of God, light will appear on the Seventh Day, and then this sophic creating of Mercury shall be completed ..."

"It is a marvellous fact that our Mercury contains active sulphur and yet preserves the form and all the properties of Mercury. Hence it is necessary that a form be introduced therein by our preparation, which form is a metallic sulphur."

"The two (the passive and the active principle) combined we call our Hermaphrodite. When joined to the Sun, it softens, liquefies, and dissolves it with gentle heat. By means of the same fire it coagulates itself; and by its coagulation produces the Sun."

At the end of some editions of *An Open Entrance to the Closed Palace of the King*, there is a small treatise entitled *Experiments: Preparations of the Sophic Mercury*. Here the Master gives useful indications that allow us to extract some conclusions about the preparation of the Philosophical Mercury. However, it was Flamel that helped us to understand the *Second Work* thanks to the annotations he made to the margins of a Psalm book, the secret of this way destined to be transmitted to his wife Perenelle's nephew.

It isn't strange, therefore, that the Master was so extremely charitable, so much in the description as also in the *modus operandi*, for he recommends his nephew to not reveal this secret to anybody:

"Remark how well you ought to operate. For if you give but little gold to the melted Saturnia, the gold is indeed opened, but the quicksilver will

not take; and here is an incongruity, which is not
at all profitable. I have a long while and greatly
laboured in this affliction, before I found out the
means to succeed in it. If therefore you give him
much gold to devour, the gold will not indeed be
so much opened nor disposed, but then it will take
the quicksilver, and they will both marry. Thus
the means is discovered. Conceal this secret, for
it is the whole, and neither trust it to paper, or to
any thing else which may be seen. For we should
become the cause of great mischief. I give it thee
under the seal of secrecy and of thy conscience, for
the love I bear thee."

Happily for us as alchemists, as it is, the *Testament* was found
by Master Dom Antoine-Joseph Pernety. Later, the nobleman
Molinier, also an alchemist, acquired Dom Pernety's copy and
he annotated carefully in the margins, the explanations that, in
their understanding, should be necessary for the execution of this
method, that he will probably also have had accomplished. Those
annotations, although a little confused and repetitive, facilitated
us much in the understanding of the different operations.

Given these explanations, we will see what Flamel refers to us
about the preparation of Philosophical Mercury.

"I tell thee, therefore, that without Sun or Moon
this work will profit thee nothing. Thou must
therefore cause this old man, or voracious wolf, to
devour gold or silver in the weight and measure as I
am now about to inform thee."

"Take thou ten ounces of the red Sun, that is to so
say, very fine, clean and purified nine or ten times
by means of the voracious wolf alone: two (*twenty
in French edition*) ounces of the royal Saturnie; melt
this in a crucible, and when it is melted, cast into it
the ten ounces of fine gold; melt these two together,

and stir them with a lighted charcoal. Then will thy gold be a little opened. Pour it on a marble slab or into an iron mortar, reduce it to a powder, and grind it well with three pounds of quicksilver. Make them to curd like cheese, in the grinding and working them to and fro: wash this amalgam with pure common water until it comes out clear, and that the whole mass appears clear and white like fine Luna. The conjunction of the gold with the royal golden Saturnie is effected, when the mass is soft to the touch like butter."

"Take this mass, which thou wilt gently dry with linen or fine cloth, with great care: this is our lead, and our mass of Sun and Moon, not the vulgar, but the philosophical. Put it into a good retort of crucible earth, but much better of steel. Place the retort in a furnace, and adapt a receiver to it: give fire by degrees. Two hours after increase your fire so that the Mercury may pass into the receiver ..."

The Master aids us with much detail, suitable indications for the preparation of the Philosophical Mercury, and comparing the proportions with the ones that Philalethes gives us we verify that there are some differences.

"The Secret of Preparing the Mercury with His Arsenic, for the Separating of its Faeces: I did take one part of the best Arsenic, and I made a marriage with two parts of the Virgin Diana into one Body; I ground it very fine, and with this I have prepared my mercury, working them all together in heat, until that they were most exquisitely incorporated: then I purged it with the Salt of Urine, that the Faeces did separate, which I put away."

Philalethes gives one part of Philosophical Arsenic and two parts of Virgin Diana. Flamel, by his side, says that they are ten parts of fine gold and twenty parts of royal Saturnie and, then, another ten parts more of fine gold.

In the *Testament* facsimile manuscript that we have there are, suitably, the following proportions, written on the margin by Molinier:

LV – 55:10 parts	= 5,5g of Sun
CX – 110:20 parts	= 5,5g of Saturnie
CLXV 165:30 parts	= 5,5g of Mercury

These proportions do not agree with those given by Philalethes and Flamel. Even so, for experimentation purpose, we thought that we could opt for the proportions annotated by the nobleman Molinier in the *Testament*.

Rightly, you will notice, the Masters give to the same materials different names. This might seem to you purposeless, but if you observe well, all the names agree with the ones that, at that time, were usual. It will require many observations to see the details here. Certainly, we easily could refer to the materials by their actual chemical designations, but then we would be giving to you for nothing that which you should have to seek for.

With relationship to the flasks used in this operation, you may find it difficult to get them just as they were constructed in past times. Therefore, you might have to manufacture them with ingeniousness yourself, or otherwise, to order them from an expert glassblower.

The union of Saturnie to the Star King or with the Virgin Diana and Venus, according to the way described, should be done in a small crucible or stainless steel container with its cover on, in a gas stove.

The *distillation* of the Philosophical Mercury should be made in a sandstone retort or, preferably, in a dismountable stainless steel retort in a sand bath. It won't be easy for you to find these indispensable retorts, so, then, you will have to order them.

The *distillation* of the Philosophical Mercury, as we said, will be carried out in a dismountable stainless steel retort, to allow for its cleaning and to remove, afterwards, the caput mortem. The receiving flask can be a 500 millilitre Pyrex glass flask, filled to half its capacity of water.

Each *distillation* of the Mercury with its Arsenic is referred to as an *Eagle*. Thus, to produce a Philosophical Mercury acceptable for the Work, it will be necessary to fly the Eagle seven to ten times, as Philalethes says:

> "But Mercury needs inward and essential purging, which radical cleansing is brought about by the addition of true Sulphur, little by little, according to the number of the Eagles."

> "The Secret of the just Preparation of the Sophic Mercury: Every single preparation of the Mercury with its Arsenic is one Eagle, the Feathers of the Eagle being purged from their Crow-like blackness, make it to fly the seventh flight, and it is prepared even until the tenth flight."

Flamel gives us more indispensable details concerning the *sublimation* of the Philosophical Mercury that Philalethes has left in the shade:

> "You may now suppose that this Mercury has eaten up a little of the body of the king, and that it will have much more strength to dissolve the other part of it hereafter, which will be more covered by the body of the Saturnie. Thou has now ascended one degree or step of the ladder of the art."

> "Take the faeces out of the retort; melt them in a crucible in a strong fire: cast into it four ounces of the Saturnie, and nine ounces of the Sun. Then the Sun is expanded in the said faeces, and much more opened that at the first time, as the Mercury has

PLATE I

Photographs by Rubellus Petrinus: (a) Iron mortar; (b) *Starry Martial Regulus*; (c) Nitre crystallisation; (d) Nitre revivification; (e) Preparation (*purification*) of Mercury; and (f) Amalgam.

PLATE II

Photographs by Rubellus Petrinus: (g) Electric stove and 2 litre alembic; (h) Native vitriol; (i) *Philosophical Egg*; (j) Salt volatilisation; (k) Tincture of Mars and Tincture of the Sun; and (l) Electric stove and 6 litre alembic.

more vigour than before, it will have the strength and virtue of penetrating the gold, and of eating more of it, and of filling his belly with it by degrees. Operate therefore as at first; marry the aforesaid Mercury, stronger one degree with this new mass in grinding the whole together; they will take like butter and cheese; wash and grind them several times, until all the blackness is got out: dry it as aforesaid; put the whole into the retort, and operate as thou didst before, by giving during two hours, a weak fire, and then strong, sufficient to drive out, and cause the Mercury to fall into the receiver; then wilt thou have the Mercury still more accuated, and thou wilt have ascended to the second degree of the philosophic ladder."

"Repeat the same work, by casting in the Saturnie in due weight, that is to say, by degrees, and operating as before, till thou hast the 10th step of the philosophic ladder; then thy rest. For the aforesaid Mercury is ignited, accuated, wholly engrossed and full of male sulphur, and fortified with the astral juice which was in the deep bowels of the gold and of our saturnine dragon. Be assured that I am now writing for thee things by no philosopher was ever declared or written."

In effect, we have never seen in any treatise this 'Eagles' operation described with so much clarity, which causes us to believe that the Master provided it deliberately, due to the circumstances that we already referred to.

The *purging* of the Philosophical Mercury has the purpose of cleaning itself of its external impurities that come from the centre to the surface and, at the same time, to introduce into it the alchemical Sulphur that it needs. As Philalethes says, this operation can be done in several ways:

"Then it also needs an incidental purgation for the purpose of removing from its surface the impurities which have, by the essential purgation, been ejected from the centre. This process is not absolutely necessary, but it is useful, as it accelerates the work."

"You may wash it with wine, or vinegar and salt, and so spare the sublimation; but then distil it at least four times without addition, after you have perfected all the eagles, or washings, washing the chalybeat retort every time with ashes and water; then boil it in distilled vinegar for half a day, stirring it strongly at times. Pour off the blackish vinegar, add new, then wash with warm water. This process is designed to purge away the internal impurities from surface. These impurities you may perceive if, on mixing Mercury with purest gold, you place the amalgam on a white sheet of paper."

"Another Purgation, but yet better: I have found out a better way of purging it, with vinegar and pure sea salt, so that in the space of half a day I can prepare one Eagle: I made the first Eagle to fly, and Diana is left, with a little tincture of brass. I began the second Eagle by removing the superfluities and then I made it fly, and again the Doves of Diana are left, with the tincture of brass. I conjoined the third Eagle, and I purged the superfluities, by removing them, even to a whiteness; then, I made it fly, and there was left a great part of brass, with the Doves of Diana. Then I made it fly twice by itself to the whole extraction of all the body. Then, I joined the fourth Eagle, by adding more and more of its own humor degrees, and there was made a very temperate consistence, in which there was no hydropsy (or superfluous moisture) as there was in the former Eagles."

With relationship to the *modus operandi*, an experienced Artist will know about the fusion of real Saturnie with the Sun or the Moon or with Diana or Venus, its amalgam with the quicksilver, the *distillation* of the Philosophical Mercury and, finally, the respective *purge*, as the Art demands.

You should have noticed that, in the *sublimation* process, the Master refers to Diana's Doves. In our understanding these Doves have no relationship to the two Doves referred to in the Philalethes *First Way*.

You will notice, also, that in order to *purge* the Philosophical Mercury it is necessary to use the spirit of vinegar and common salt. We have already previously mentioned this and we repeat it here again, that the salts used in the alchemic operations, in this case the sodium chloride, shall be always of natural origin. The same is applied to the spirits. Thus, the Artist from pure wine vinegar shall distill the spirit of vinegar.

The spirit of vinegar has other applications in our Art, as we will see ahead, and all alchemists should be aware of this as they carry out, themselves, the canonical *distillation* of this spirit, as well as that of the spirit of wine.

We can advise that the *distillation* of the spirit of vinegar, of itself, is a true Herculean work, because to obtain 5 litres of spirit at 10 degrees Baume, you will need to distill, at least, 50 or 60 litres of strong wine vinegar at 10 percent by volume. Besides this, it is necessary to possess the manual skill required to correctly carry out this operation, which only an expert alchemist knows.

If you understood well that which Philalethes and Flamel charitably transmitted to us in their books, and which we have included here in the Work's sequence to facilitate understanding of the texts and the *modus operandi*, then you will be capable of trying out the preparation of the Philosophical Mercury, that will allow you to start the *Third Work*. If that was not possible for you it is likely because you don't yet have the necessary knowledge, and you aren't properly prepared to enter in the Sanctuary of our Art.

THE THIRD WORK

In the *Second Work* we made the conjugation of common quicksilver with the Sun or the Moon or with the Moon or Venus, through real Saturnie, in the proportions recommended by Philalethes and Flamel, with a view to it being philosophical and suitable for the Work.

In the *Third Work* we will proceed, first, to the *sublimation* and *purgation* of the Philosophical Mercury in order to purify it. Consecutively, it will be amalgamated with the solar star in the proper proportions, and finally, cooking the amalgam in a closed *Philosophical Egg*, in an oven named an athanor.

Let us see, then, what Philalethes tells us in *An Open Entrance to the Closed Palace of the King*, about the *purification* and *sublimation* of the Philosophical Mercury.

The Master teaches several processes for purifying it and it would be annoying to refer to them all, because the process is practically the same each time, with some variants. Therefore we recommend to those who are interested, to read the Chapter XV and XVI of *An Open Entrance to the Closed Palace of the King*. Thus we have transcribed that which, from our experience, seemed to us the most useful.

> "Therefore, take your Mercury, which you have purified with a suitable number of Eagles, sublime it three times with common salt and iron filings, and wash it with vinegar and a moderate quantity of salts of ammonia, then dry and distil in a glass retort, over a gradually increasing fire, until the whole of the Mercury has ascended. Repeat this four times, then boil the Mercury in spirits of vinegar for an hour, stirring it constantly. Then

pour off the vinegar, and wash off its acidity by a plentiful effusion of spring water. Dry the Mercury, and its splendour will be wonderful."

"When you have done all this, take one part of pure and laminated gold, or fine gold filings, and two parts of Mercury; put them in a heated (marble) jar, i.e. heaved with boiling water, being taken out of which it dries quickly, and holds the heat a long time. Grind with an ivory, or glass, or stone, or iron, or boxwood pestle (*the iron pestle is not so good; I use a pestle of crystal*): pound them, I say, as small as the painters grind their colours; then add water so as to make the mass as consistent as half melted butter. The mixture should be fixable and soft, and permit itself to be moulded into little globules – like moderately soft butter; it should be of such a consistency as to yield to the gentlest touch. Moreover, it should be of the same temperature throughout, and one part should not be more liquid than another. The mixture will be more or less soft, according to the proportion of Mercury which it contains; but it must be capable of forming into those little globules, and the Mercury should not be more lively at the bottom than at the top."

"Then take spirit of vinegar, and dissolve in it a third part of salt of ammonia, put the amalgam into this liquid, let the whole boil for a quarter-of-an-hour in a long necked glass vessel; then take the mixture out of the glass vessel, pour off the liquid, heat the mortar, and pound the amalgam (as above) vigorously, and wash away all blackness with hot water. Put it again into the liquid, let it boil up once more in the glass vessel, pound it as before, and wash it. Repeat this process until the blackness is entirely purged out. The amalgam will then be as brilliant and white as the purest silver (see Plate I-f)."

Flamel, in his *Testament*, is practically silent on this operation and passes directly to the amalgam just as it will be constituted and placed in the *Philosophical Egg*, different again than Philalethes indicates, although the final results are similar.

> "Learn therefore and observe well how to operate, in the manner I am about to relate to you. In the name of God, thou shalt take of thy animated Mercury what quantity thou pleasest; thou wilt put it into a glass vessel by itself; or two or four parts of the Mercury with two parts of the golden Saturnie; that is to say, one of the Sun and two of the Saturnie; the whole finely conjoined like butter, washed, cleansed and dried; and thou wilt lute thy vessel with the lute of wisdom. Place it in a furnace on warm ashes at the degree of the heat of an hen sitting on her eggs. Leave this said Mercury so prepared to ascend and descend for the space of 40 or 50 days, until thou sees forming in thy vessel a white or red sulphur, called philosophic sublimate, which issues out of the reins of the said Mercury. Thou wilt collect this sulphur with a feather: it is the living Sun and the living Moon, which Mercury begets out of itself."

Philalethes is very meticulous in the description that arrives at the point of explaining the *Philosophical Egg* (see Plate II-i) and the furnace. As it won't be possible for you to buy, ready made, a flask the same as the one he describes, unavoidably, you will have to order it to be made by a master glassblower.

In relation to the oven, today we have other different and much cleaner technical resources more practical than the one our past Masters used. Some think that the fuel source should be natural, that is, coal or butane gas. Others affirm that electrical heating, being more practical and cleaner, will accomplish the purpose just as effectively.

With relation to this point, effectively, the heat of an incandescent metallic resistance, produced by electrical alternate current, is effective in most cases, especially because the temperature can almost be regulated by the exact degree. However, there is the radiation provoked by the electromagnetic field in the referred resistance, which might be harmful to the Work in certain cases. We don't have confirmation of this. However, experience will show you the best solution.

Let us see, now, what Philalethes says about the cooking flask:

> "Let your glass distilling vessel be round or oval; large enough to hold neither more nor much less than an ounce of distilled water in the body thereof. Let the height of the vessel's neck be about one palm, hand-breath, or span, and let the glass be clear and thick (the thicker the better, so long as it is clean, and permits you distinguish what is going on within) but the thickness should be uniform. The substance which will go into this vessel consists of ½ oz. of gold, and 1 oz. of mercury; and if you have to add ⅓ oz. of mercury, the whole compound will still be less than 2 oz. The glass should be strong in order to prevent the vapours, which arise from our embryo, bursting the vessel. Let the mouth of the vessel be very carefully and effectually secured by means of thick layer of sealing-wax."

> "When you have prepared our gold and Mercury in the manner described, put it into our vessel, and subject it to the action of fire; within 40 days you will see the whole substance converted into atoms,

without any visible motion, or perceptible heat (except that it is just warm)."

Certainly, you may notice that Philalethes refers to two different ways of operating, and, therefore, it generates a great confusion with the text's interpretation. In the first he says:

"The substance which will go into this vessel consists of ½ oz. of gold, and 1 oz. of mercury ..."

And in the other:

"When you have prepared our gold (Sun) and Mercury in the manner described ..."

Before we explain the difference between the two different operations, we will refer back a little, to Chapter XI, 'Concerning the Discovery of the Perfect Magistery,' of *An Open Entrance to the Closed Palace of the King*:

"Mercury emerged in a hermaphroditic state. Then they placed it in the fire; in no long time they succeeded in coagulating, and in its coagulation they found the Sun and Moon in a most pure state."

And, to complete this analysis, we will also mention Flamel:

"In the name of God, thou shalt take of thy animated Mercury what quantity thou pleasest; thou wilt put it into a glass vessel by itself; or two or four parts of the Mercury with two parts of the golden Saturnie; that is to say, one of the Sun and two of the Saturnie; the whole finely conjoined like butter, washed, cleansed and dried ..."

What can we conclude from what here was said? That the Philosophical Mercury, *per se*, placed in a closed flask and by applying a suitable heat, becomes Sun or Moon, according to the luminary with which it was married; that is, it becomes Philosophical Sulphur, or *Our Gold*.

In the second case, the common purified Sun or Moon, cooked in our Mercury, also becomes Philosophical Sulphur. We can work by either of these two processes because, according to the texts, the result is the same.

Here it is, dear Brothers of the Art, the mystery of *Our Sun* that Philalethes refers to in his book and that has provoked so much confusion in certain Iberian alchemic Artists.

After the amalgam has been put into a suitable flask (*Egg*), it is placed in a philosophical oven called an athanor, to be cooked at the different heat levels.

Philalethes, in his book, refers to seven levels, as follows: *Mercury, Saturn, Jupiter, Moon, Venus, Mars,* and *Sun*. It would be very annoying to describe them all when you can study them yourselves in detail in Philalethes' *An Open Entrance to the Closed Palace of the King*. Therefore, we refer just to Flamel's way, it being the most comprehensible.

Flamel, as it was already mentioned above, recommends picking up, with a feather, the white and red Sulphur, because they are the living gold and the living silver (*Our Gold* and *Our Silver*).

Then, in the final parts of his *Testament*, he recommends the operation, as in the following:

> "Take this white or red sulphur, triturate it in a glass or marble mortar, and pour on it, in sprinkling it, a third part of its weight of Mercury from which this sulphur has been drawn. With these two make a paste like butter: put again this mixture into oval glass; place it in a furnace on a suitable fire of ashes, mild, and disposed with a philosophic industry. Concoct until the said Mercury is changed into sulphur, and during this concoction, thou wilt see wonderful things in the vessel, that is to say, all the

colours which exist in the world, which thou canst
not behold without lifting up thy heart to God in
gratitude for so great a gift."

"When thou has attained to the purple red, thou
must gather it: for then the alchemical powder is
made, transmuting every metal into fine pure and
neat gold, which thou maist multiply by watering
it as thou hast already done, grinding it with fresh
Mercury, concocting it in the same vessel, furnace
and fire, and the time will be much shorter, and its
virtue ten times stronger."

Consecutively, Flamel refers to another way of operating, that
is, with the gold, without the white and red Sulfur (*Our Gold*).

"Shouldest thou desire to operate in another way,
take of fine Sun in fine powder or in very thin leaves:
make a paste for it with 7 parts of thy philosophic
Mercury, which is our Luna: put them both into an
oval glass vessel well luted; place it in a furnace;
give a very strong fire, that is to say, such as will
keep lead in fusion; for then thou has found out the
true regimen of fire; and let thy Mercury, which
is the philosophical wind, ascend and descend on
the body of the gold, which it eats up by degrees,
and carries in its belly. Concoct it until the gold
and Mercury do no more ascend and descend, but
both remain quiet, and then will peace and union
be effected between the two dragons, which are fire
and water both together."

"Then wilt thou see in thy vessel a great blackness
like of melted pitch, which is the sign of death
and putrefaction of the gold, and the key of the
whole Magistery. Cause it therefore to resuscitate
by concocting it (40 days), and be not weary with

concocting it: during this period diverse changes
will take place; that is to say, the matter will pass
through all colours, the black, the ash colour, the
blue, the green, the white, the orange, and finally
the red as red as blood or the crimson poppy: aim
only at this last colour; for this is the true sulphur,
and alchemical powder."

It is quite evident, then, as Philalethes says, and as is also
confirmed by Flamel, that there are two different ways to operate:
one with *Our Gold* or Sulphur produced from the concoction and
coagulation of the Philosophical Mercury in a closed flask and, the
other, concocting and coagulating *Our Water* in the *Philosophical
Egg* with common gold. Both ways are equivalent; the only
difference being that this last one is more expensive.

Here, then, is the *Projection Powder*; our red Sulphur that is
necessary to *multiply*; to increase its transmutative power.

"If thou are disposed to multiply thy powder, take
one part thereof, and water it with two parts of thy
animated Mercury; make it into a soft and smooth
paste; put it in a vessel as thou hast already done,
in the same furnace and fire, and concoct it. This
second turn of the philosophic wheel will be done
in less time than the first, and thy powder will have
ten times more strength. Let it wheel about again
a thousand times, and as much as thou wilt. Thou
wilt then have a treasure without price, superior
to all there is in the world, and thou canst desire
nothing more here below, for thou both health and
riches, if you useth them properly."

The *fermentation* which proceeds is made by concocting, in a
closed glass vessel, an amalgam of three parts of powdered fine
gold with six parts of living Mercury and a part and a half of red
Sulphur.

To use the *Universal Medicine* for the health of the body, some few grains are diluted in white wine or liquor, until the wine is coloured, just tinctured slightly, because this tincture is the sign of measure. Give to a patient 12-15 drops in wine, or in another liquor, and as if by a miracle, he, as Flamel says, will be cured.

Finally, the *transmutation* is as proceeds. We recommend students to read the *Testament* in the chapter that describes preparation of the *Projection Powder*, starting from the Elixir. Also Philalethes, in *An Open Entrance to the Closed Palace of the King*, explains in plain language how a *transmutation* is performed.

We here finish our commentary on the Philalethes and Flamel *Amalgam Path*. The curious reader will probably be interested in interrogating us to see if that which we describe here is true. Up to the present we can confirm its truthfulness to the point where we have arrived in this document, thanks to the charitable teachings of these Masters. We will continue, without faintheartedness, our way. With the help of God, we will reach the end.

We don't fear critics or detractors, because what we have written and have tried is true.

To our knowledge no modern alchemist dared go so far towards divulging, in writing, the work of these two alchemists. As we explained in the beginning of this treatise, we have done this with the intention of demonstrating to the skeptic that alchemy continues to live and that this Art which the Masters have written about is a perennial tradition, for we today know how to interpret them. It is evident that we are not allowed to say everything we would like to about alchemy, mainly in respects to the operative details, because those are the occult 'keys' to the work.

However, we will be satisfied if some of you, Brothers that love Hermes' Art, find in this modest work enough teaching to allow you to travel your own way.

THE GREAT ALCHEMICAL WORK OF

Basil Valentine: Part One

Portrait of Basil Valentine from the title page of his *Revelation des mysteres* (Paris, 1668).

There has been written, and continues to be written, too much about alchemy, mainly with respect to its historic and occult aspects. There are many commentators on alchemy in this world, some of whom understand nothing of alchemy, and therefore being limited in their writings, speculate about the meaning of some alchemical allegories without sense of the practical aspects of the Art, transcribing texts that, in their greatest part, are arid like the desert sand and don't relate to any true alchemical Path.

This might be accepted easily, given the immense difficulty there exists in the interpretation of known classic texts.

To approach alchemy conscientiously under its interpretative and practical aspect, it is necessary to have much knowledge not only of the terminology used by the old Masters in their books, but also of the several materials spoken of, and of the actual *modus operandi*.

We recognise that this is very difficult, especially with the positivist mentality and its actual scientific knowledge. We need, then, to return to the 17-19th centuries in this respect, and to the knowledge of the chemistry, mineralogy and the arts of that time.

This is not an easy task, because it requires many years of investigation of the classic literature of our Artistic study and of other kindred books.

In our country we are fortunate in this aspect, because there exists in our public libraries not only technical and scientific books from that time, even some in French, as well as the primary classic alchemical works of the great Masters.

Unhappily these treatises were mostly written in Latin. We say unhappily because knowledge of Latin isn't always accessible to all people, including ourselves.

However, it is of great worth to us that there is on the international market alchemical and scientific books of that time, many of which are in French.

The curious reader and the lover of our Art will, in his quest, find it is pertinent that he has knowledge of chemistry in order to understand and practice alchemy.

There exist a lot of divergent opinions about this subject in our times. We, for example, understand that it is necessary to have at least some knowledge of ancient chemistry (spagyrics), as it was practiced in past ages, to understand the *modus operandi* of alchemy.

It is evident that we can work in alchemy without knowing any chemistry, it being enough, in practice, to follow the directions given by the instructor, or through the Master, about any particular operations. However, the technical foundation of alchemy, in our opinion, can never be understood properly, if we do not know what chemical reactions may occur between the materials involved.

There are those who affirm that this way of thinking is simply the ego's indulgence. We don't generally accept this simplistic assertion, and suggest that it probably conceals a weakness of knowledge in this area.

This brings to mind a situation that happened to us, some 20 years previously; we being still at the peak of our youth, at a time when we just obtained our pilot's license. At the end of instruction we asked the instructor, who in fact was more of an airplane 'driver' than an airplane pilot, why the plane, an old and tired out Piper Super Cruiser, in which we flew, hadn't gone to the Devil before now? Then one day the motor stopped during flight without us knowing the distance the airplane could glide according to the altitude we were at. Embarrassed with the question at hand, because he didn't know the answer, it caused a forced smile to appear upon the face of the instructor, after giving the evasive answer: "So you think it is necessary to know this in order to land safely?"

We did not answer him and had swallowed our pride because we knew that if we pressed him further, we would end up in conflict with our instructor.

We were constrained by our preference for continuing to learn, even inside the limitations that were imposed on us by our instructor.

With respect to learning alchemy we came across similar circumstances. We saw many smiles, which betrayed a hypocritical wisdom, that were no more than masks that thinly disguised their ignorance. It is to break the ego ... they say on behalf of obscure theories that have nothing to do with the alchemical Tradition, and that were never professed by the true Masters of the royal Art.

It is also true to say that in alchemy there are things that don't have an easily comprehensible and possible explanation, but that is another thing altogether.

But, we assert, this is part of the way of learning of our Art. It is necessary to understand that obedience and humility should not be confused with subservience and alienation. Above all, the need for much perseverance must be recognised.

Don't feel that one can learn alchemy by the reading of books alone, even if they are the best classic or contemporary authors. Be disappointed by all those that think like this, because they will be unavoidably enticed onto the wrong path. If you don't progress by means of a Master or Brother in the Art's charitable hand, you will never make headway, unless they provide knowledge of at least the first steps.

Unhappily, today it is not easy to find a Master. In relationship to Brothers in the Art, they are also rare and not every one will be disposed to help fraternally, even recognising the honesty of those that ask help of them.

Some of these Brothers that, by tradition, should be charitable, either through their books or in their teachings, are, on the contrary, closed in an egocentrism that they should be intending to combat.

Of the contemporary authors, there are the erudite, whose works of incontestably historical value, are just valuable auxiliaries in the Art's research.

Amongst the erudite, there are also those who, besides historical facts, reveal great knowledge of the Hermetic Art; much at the theoretical level, as well as at the practical. Therefore, those works are invaluable jewels amongst alchemical literature. However, some of those books that seem to first impressions so seductive, are, on the contrary, extremely closed.

Should we conclude that most of the alchemical books are like this? We think not. We were errant for plenty of years because of the tortuous ways that were marked by some false prophets, and even by some of the erudite. Their books were filled with beautiful speeches and with simple dialectics, at times deceitful. In transcribing excerpts from texts mutilated in their essentials by being removed from their context, they have made more difficult the way for neophytes, forcing them to spend, in vain work, years of their lives wandering in the desert of despair.

It was good for us though, at least, to read some such works in the hope of finding some luminary reported, to shed some light however pale, that didn't leave us completely in the darkness.

Through an act of charity, these works sometimes also indicated, with some exactitude, the sources from which we may satiate our thirst; sources which, most often were not very accessible. Of those sources there was a need to distinguish the drinkable water from the polluted, and it was with much perseverance that we came, after more than 20 years, to distinguish the bad from the very bad, and the bearable from the good.

Nevertheless, through all the difficulties, little by little, we came to acquire the great Master's classic works, which we studied with much interest.

Finally, we managed to find some light that allowed us to begin the first practical processes. After countless experiments patiently repeated, some not totally exempt of risk, we were able to verify, with satisfaction, that the chemical operations (spagyrical) referred to allegorically in those books, had real meaning and they provided us with practical results.

We found multiple difficulties in the books of these Hermetic

'Masters.' Thus wise, for you, Brothers and lovers of our Art that read us, in order to go further in outlining some of the obstacles, we have written this modest work as a beacon for you to find the way at least upon the path that we travelled.

The symbology of the spagyrics of that time was created practically anew at each individual Artist's discretion, although some uniformity already existed with the main symbolism.

Working conditions are a great obstacle in the practice of alchemy. It isn't easy in an apartment or flat (and how many can afford a house?) to provide a retreat where we can work without risk to the people that inhabit the same home. There are operations that cannot be carried out under such conditions, because they demand an oven that operates with temperatures of about one thousand degrees and, also, some of the materials that are necessary to manipulate exhale toxic fumes.

However, with the *Humid Method* it will often be possible to work under such living conditions, because the chemical reactions usually are carried out in closed Pyrex glass flasks or in retorts, with moderate temperatures.

We have already said that it is necessary to have some knowledge of spagyrics and of alchemical symbology to understand the true alchemical books. Anyone can verify this statement easily if they read one of these books.

Without a doubt we will see that there are things that seemingly don't make much practical sense, as in: "the hungry wolf that eats the Sun," the fight among the "rooster and the fox," of the "Dragon and of the Eagle," of "the warrior Mars and of the Black Dragon," etc.

We can affirm without any fear of deceiving people that this allegorical language makes sense because, usually, it designates chemical or mineral materials that take part in various operations.

It is licit also that the reader might ask if those operations, described symbolically, with much accuracy, mean something practical in an alchemical context.

We would answer yes, and further, we will give some examples of this to demonstrate to the skeptic that alchemy is something more than the philosophical speculation that frequently is found in some of the books about our Art.

Of the known classic works, among others, we have always had a very special fascination for the books of the great Master that was Basil Valentine.

Basil Valentine was a monk belonging to the Benedictine Order of St. Peter of Erfurt, and he lived at the beginning of the 15th century. It seems his name was a nom de plume that means 'powerful King.'

It was said that his writings were found under a marble table of the principal altar of a church, in the imperial city of Erfurt; he having left them there to be found by somebody that Nature had blessed.

And it is said that a bolt of lightning knocked down the church wall, and so the texts were uncovered.

Basil Valentine is one of the most well known, and also one of the most controversial, alchemists.

His writings are incisive and also harsh, not saving to criticise the doctors and 'puffers' of his time.

His more famous books are *Azoth, ou Le moyen de faire l'or caché des Philosophes, The Triumphal Chariot of Antimony, Twelve Keys* and, finally, *The Last Will and Testament.*

We spent many years studying and trying to decipher the illustrations in *Twelve Keys*, one of the most difficult books of the Master to comprehend, and which was translated into French and commented upon by the erudite contemporary scholar of the Art, Eugène Canseliet. It is some of those illustrations that we now intend to comment on. Not their esoteric and symbolic meaning that, for better or worse, has already been looked at; but on their practical meaning. It is a daring task because, as far as we know, until now, nobody has attempted to do this.

THE FIRST KEY

King on the left and a Queen on the right stand in an open landscape. The King holds a scepter in his right hand the Queen holds a three-blossomed flower in her right and a peacock feather fan in her left. In front of the King a wolf or dog jumps over a triangular crucible placed on a basin of fire. In front of the Queen, an old man with a scythe and a crippled leg (a Saturnian figure) steps across a fire on which a vessel (cupel) is being heated.

Eugène Canseliet's comments on the first figure in the French edition are as follows:

> "The King and the Queen of the Work, that is, the gold and the philosophical silver, spagyrically designated by the wolf and the great metallic button on the cupel. These and the crucible in the middle of the flames, indicate clearly the dry way, in which represents a great role the secret fire ..."

Albert Poisson in his book *Théories & Symboles des Alchimistes, Le Grand Œuvre* (page 87), says:

> "The gold and the purified silver constitute the stone's remote matter. The Sulphur is extracted from gold, the Mercury from silver, being the close matter."

We will describe, now, the text of the First Key in its more essential parts:

> "Let my friend know that no impure or spotted things are useful for our purpose. For there is nothing in their leprous nature capable of

The First Key of Basil Valentine: Above, engraving from Michael Maier's *Tripus aureus* (1618), and below, earlier reversed variant.

advancing the interests of our Art. There is much more likelihood of that which is in itself good being spoiled by that which is impure. Everything that is obtained from the mines has its value, unless, indeed, it is adulterated. Adulteration, however, spoils its goodness and its efficacy."

"As the physician purges and cleanses the inward parts of the body, and removes all unhealthy matter by means of his medicines, so our metallic substances must be purified and refined of all foreign matter, in order to ensure the success of our task. Therefore, our Masters require a pure, immaculate body, that is untainted with any foreign admixture, which admixture is the leprosy of our metals."

"Let the diadem of the King be of pure gold, and let the Queen that is united to him in wedlock be chaste and immaculate."

"If you would operate by means of our bodies, take a fierce grey wolf, which, though on account of its name it be subject to the sway of warlike Mars, is by birth the offspring of ancient Saturn, and is found in the valleys and mountains of the world, where he roams about savage with hunger. Cast to him the body of the King, and when he has devoured it, burn him entirely to ashes in a great fire. By this process the King will be liberated; and when it has been performed thrice the Lion has overcome the wolf, and will find nothing more to devour in him. Thus our Body has been rendered fit for the first stage of our work."

"Know that this is the only right and legitimate way of purifying our substance: for the Lion purifies himself with the blood of the wolf, and the tincture

of its blood agrees most wonderfully with the
tincture of the Lion, seeing that the two liquids are
closely akin to each other."

"But let my friend be scrupulously careful to
preserve the fountain of life limpid and clear. If any
strange water be mixed with it, it is spoiled, and
becomes positively injurious."

"The King travels through six regions in the heavenly
firmament, and in the seventh he fixes his abode.
There the royal palace is adorned with golden
tapestry. If you understand my meaning, this Key
will open the first lock, and push the first bolt; but
if you do not, no spectacles or natural eyesight will
enable you to understand what follows."

In the French edition:

"Because if truly, you understood the light of my
words, there are not glasses that advance you, nor
natural eyes that help you, so that you find in the
end that lacked you at the beginning ..."

It tends, in the account Canseliet gives, and also in that of
Albert Poisson, in reference to the woodcut images, to cause us to
conclude that the King represents the gold that will be purified by
the wolf, and the Queen the silver. Also Saturn purifies it in the
cupel as you can see from the metallic button. This *purification*
method of these two noble metals was very common at that time.

This is a possible interpretation, which, at first view, seems the
most suitable, and, for some time, we accepted this but with some
reservation.

If you read carefully the text of this Key, you will see that
the Master does not make any reference to the *purification* of the
Queen. He refers only to the King's *purification*, and it is from
there that our doubt springs forth.

We never accepted willingly the comments of the translator and commentator, an erudite man, author of several books about our Art – that we respected much – because they don't agree with the text and we found it very strange that he didn't repair what seemed to be obvious mistakes.

Later, we acquired *The Last Will and Testament*, one of Basil Valentine's last published books. As the title suggests, it will probably have been the Master's last book and perhaps because of this, one of the most generous and clear.

In the work referred to, we confirm our reservations because the Master describes there in plain language some of the keys of his book *Twelve Keys* which, in the original, were described in symbolic language.

Let us see, then, what the Master tells about the First Key in *The Last Will and Testament*:

> "The first Key informs you that if you seek for the seed in a metalline body, as in the gold ..."

> "This purifying is performed with Antimony, which stands in a near relation, and affinity unto Gold, which is the reason, why antimonial Sulphur purges the Soul of Gold, graduating the same to a very high degree ..."

> "The purifying of the gold is performed thus: Laminate the gold thinly, after a due manner, cast it thrice through Antimony, afterwards the REGULUS which is set at the through casting, must be melted before the blast in a strong fire, and driven off with SATURN, then you will find the purest, fairest, most lustrous Gold, pleasant to behold, as much as lustre of SOL is."

The text is clear and it doesn't leave place for any doubt. The King and only the King is purified by antimony or the grey wolf (the wolf jumping over the crucible) and, then, in the cupel by

Saturn (the old man with a crippled leg and a scythe), having a cupel under him with a metallic button of purified gold, as shown in the figure.

As the Key's text points out, Saturn is the seventh region in the celestial firmament (seventh alchemical planet). The wolf represents, symbolically, antimony and Saturn, lead.

The old Masters, when referring to antimony meant, respectively, the mineral that is called stibnite or the natural sulphide of antimony. In order to distinguish the mineral of the metal they designated it as the *Regulus of Antimony*.

Let us see, now, how gold was *purged* by the Artists of the 17th century, as it is described in the *Traité De La Chymie* (1667, page 84) of Christophle Glaser, an ordinary chemist of the French King:

> "The purification of the gold for the antimony. The best purification of gold is that which is made by antimony; lead only destroys the imperfect metals and it leaves silver with the gold; cement frequently leaves the impure gold and it still eats it a small portions; quartation does not always prove the test of the purity of gold ... it can make sure that the gold that goes by antimony is purged and freed perfectly of all impurity, because there is no gold that can resist this devouring wolf."

> "Take, therefore, one ounce of gold, just as goldsmiths use it, place it in a crucible among burning charcoal, in a fire facing the wind, and, as soon as it is red-hot, pour in, little by little, four ounces of good powdered antimony, which will melt immediately and it will devour the gold at the same time, which, by any other way, such a melt it is difficult to obtain, because of gold's very perfect composition. Now that everything is melted like water and that the matter has sparks lying within it, it is a sign that the action of the antimony has

destroyed the impurities of the gold and that it is necessary to still leave it a little in the fire and, then, to drain it quickly into a steel mould that has been previously warm and greased with oil."

"As soon as the material is drained into the mould, it is at the same time necessary to beat the mould with hammer and tongs, so as to help the regulus to move down into the bottom of the mould."

"After the matter is cool, it is necessary to separate the regulus from caput mortem, to weigh it and afterwards to place it in a crucible to melt it, pouring in, little by little, double its weight in nitre; close the crucible with its cover, so that coal can't enter in and, giving it a strong fire, the nitre will consume all of the antimony that still remains."

"The gold is then found melted in the bottom, very beautiful and pure. It can be drained into a steel mould or can be left to cool in the crucible, which it will be necessary to break, then, to separate the gold from the salts."

It seems to us that it is not necessary to be an expert in metallurgy to understand this operation with gold, or, what we call, the King's *purification* by antimony, and therefore it does not require any further comment by us.

In the first part of this book ('The Great Alchemical Work of Eirenaeus Philalethes and Nicholas Flamel'), we have referred to nitre already and, also, to its canonical preparation.

To conclude our comment on the First Key, we summarise: the *purification* of gold (the King) is made in a crucible of refractory ceramic, in a gas oven, by natural antimony sulphide (stibnite), powdered, which the old alchemists denominated a 'hungry grey wolf' (because it devours any metal), melting it with the gold. After melting it, it is drained into a previously oiled or greased steel mould. Separate the *Solar Regulus* from the caput mortem and put it, after roughly grinding it, into a crucible with twice its weight in nitre. Make a very strong fire and melt the regulus with the nitre, so that it consumes the remaining antimony.

Finally, Saturn (lead) purifies the gold in a cupel. Thereafter we find remaining in the cupel a button of very pure gold.

Do we now ask, what is the reason, in the image of the First Key, for the appearance of the Queen and the King together, if she isn't referred to in the text, nor is attributed any role at this point?

We do have an answer here. We know of another version of the *Twelve Keys*, whose woodcuts are not as perfectly executed and, therefore, they seem to us to be older, which we have also inserted in the present book; versions that, in the more recent editions, appear reversed.

To our understanding, there is an explanation for this. The *Twelve Keys* was first published in 1599 without illustrations, and in 1602 with some woodcuts of the Twelve Keys. So, the woodcuts were placed in the body of the text by another person who was not the original author.

The explanation of the text that we have given was made, deliberately, in plain language. In alchemy it is not usual to do this. But if the Master, through his charity, did so in *The Last Will and Testament*, for what reason would we not do likewise?

THE SECOND KEY

This key refers to the preparation of the King's bath, that is to say, the preparation of a solvent water for the Solar Star. In the woodcut of the Second Key, winged Mercury stands holding a caduceus in each hand. To the left is the Sun and to the right the Moon, and at his feet a set of double wings. Approaching him from the left is a man with a sword around which a serpent or snake coils; while from the right is another man with a sword, upon the point of which a bird perches.

Canseliet's comment on the Second Key in the French edition is as follows:

> "This is an expressive image of the Bride of the Great Work, substituting it for a young nude man, winged and crowned, young Mercury and a small king, as they attest to the two caduceus – where the stick has given place to the sovereign's scepter. He was born of the sun and of the philosopher's moon because they are fighting the two fencers and, thanks to these, he wins in beauty, in purity, what he loses through the heterogeneous feces in volatility. This is what is expressed by the large abandoned wings lying extended on the ground."

In agreement with the illustration and according to the commentary, the symbolism doesn't seem to us difficult to interpret: the *Philosophical Mercury* (young winged man) is obtained by the solvent's action on the first matter. The resulting water – the two fencers fighting (two opposing chemical substances), one fixed and penetrating (serpent) and the other volatile (eagle) – is also the bathing of the Sun and of the Moon.

The Second Key of Basil Valentine: Above, engraving from Michael Maier's *Tripus aureus* (1618), and below, earlier reversed variant.

Let us see, now, what the text says of the Second Key in its more essential part:

> "In the same way our bridal pair, Apollo and Diana, are arrayed in splendid attire, and their heads and bodies are washed with various kinds of water, some strong, some weak, but not one of them exactly the same as another, each designed for its own special purpose"

> "But you should notice that the King and his spouse must be quite naked when they are joined together. They must be stripped of all their glorious apparel, and must lie down together in the same state of nakedness in which they were born, that their seed may not be spoiled by being mixed with any foreign matter."

> "Let me tell you, in conclusion, that the bath in which the bridegroom is placed, must consist of two hostile kinds of matter, that purge and rectify each other by means of a continued struggle. For it is not good for the Eagle to build her nest on the summit of the Alps, because her young ones are thus in great danger of being frozen to death by the intense cold that prevails there."

> "But if you add to the Eagle the icy Dragon that has long had its habitation upon the rocks, and has crawled forth from the caverns of the earth, and place both over the fire, it will elicit from the icy Dragon a fiery spirit, which, by means of its great heat, will consume the wings of the Eagle, and prepare a perspiring bath of so extraordinary a degree of heat that the snow will melt upon the summit of the mountains, and become a water, with which the invigorating mineral bath may be

>prepared, and fortune, health, life, and strength
>restored to the King."

If you read carefully this excerpt from the text, you will verify
that, in the beginning, the Master refers to the engagement
of Apollo and Diana and the waters with which they should be
washed. Already, at the end, he says, with all truth, that the
water, an invigorating mineral bath, is prepared so that it gives to
the King fortune and health.

It is evident that his speech has changed. He starts out referring
to Apollo and Diana's engagement and finishes advising us that
the mineral bath is prepared, so that it might give to the King
fortune and health.

This is in agreement with the First Key, because, as we saw, the
described *purification* refers only to the King, that is, to the gold.

Finally, Basil Valentine tells us how the water will be prepared
for the King's bath:

>"But if you add to the Eagle the icy Dragon that
>has long had its habitation upon the rocks, and
>has crawled forth from the caverns of the earth,
>and place both over the fire, it will elicit from the
>icy Dragon a fiery spirit, which, by means of its
>great heat, will consume the wings of the Eagle,
>and prepare a perspiring bath of so extraordinary
>a degree of heat that the snow will melt upon the
>summit of the mountains, and become a water,
>with which the invigorating mineral bath may be
>prepared, and fortune, health, life, and strength
>restored to the King."

Transposing this for our spagyric language, the Serpent (Dragon)
represents the *nitre*, and the Eagle the *ammonium salt*. Therefore,
the water referred to should be prepared by a hot reaction, in the
bowl of a Pyrex-glass retort, of two contrary chemical substances,
one fixed (nitre) and the other volatile (ammonium salt), both
very well known by the old alchemists.

These two substances, mixed in proportions āā (equal parts), poured by successive fractions into the retort, when they enter into contact, with heat supplied by a stove with controlled temperature by means of a sand bath, a violent chemical reaction will be produced that will cause to distill, through the retort beak, a sudorific water that has the property of dissolving gold or the King, known by the name of *Royal Water*.

We don't want to leave off here without pointing out, with due respect, to all those that, through curiosity or in order to confirm what we said, desire to prepare this solvent water by the method indicated by the Master in this key, to abstain from making it if they do not have lab experience and have not gained the indispensable skill required in the manual techniques – otherwise, they would be exposing themselves to a great danger, because the retort can explode from an excess of pressure caused by the rapid expansion of internal gases. After the chemical reaction has started between these two belligerent salts it is uncontrollable and it could immediately break the retort, provoking serious burns if the substances come into contact with your body.

The technique to observe, as we already said, is to pour little by little into the retort bowl small amounts of the material, and immediately replace the retort's stopper.

We don't want, through negligence or inexperience, anything bad to happen to you. Alchemy, just as with chemistry, has its risks that are necessary to acknowledge, in order to avoid or to minimise them.

Besides, it is not required to take unnecessary risks, because other less dangerous methods exist for preparing this water, as we will see further on.

There is no doubt, and those who know will agree, that alchemy is a true Art, as we have already demonstrated earlier in 'The Great Alchemical Work of Eirenaeus Philalethes and Nicholas Flamel,' as with the explanation of the First and, now, the Second Key.

But we digress; let us continue to verify a divergence between this Key's text and its pictorial symbolism.

The Second Key's illustration shows us symbolically which chemical substances are necessary for the preparation of the solvent water, as well as the goal – with this purpose: the obtaining and *purification* of the Philosophical Mercury. But we already know, and in the text it is very clear, that the purpose of this water is found in the bathing of the King (dissolution), with view to the extraction of its *Mercury*, of its *Salt* and, mainly, of its alchemical *Sulphur*.

Let us see, now, what Basil Valentine says in *The Last Will and Testament* about the Second Key:

> "My friend note, and take that into a serious consideration, because the chiefest point lyes herein; cause a Balneum to be made, let nothing come into it, which should not be there, that the noble seed of the Gold fall not into a destructive and irrecoverable opposition after its destruction, and take an exact and careful view of such things, which my second Key informs you of, namely what matter you ought to take to the KINGS BALNEUM, whereby the KING is destroyed, and its external form broken, and its undefiled Soul may come forth, to this purpose will serve the DRAGON and the EAGLE, which is NITRE and SAL ARMONIACK (ammonium salt), both which after their union are made into a AQUAFORT (*Royal Water*), as you shall be further informed of in my Manuals, where I shall treat in particular of Gold, of other Metals and Minerals, into which BALNEUM the King is thrown, being first, as in the quoted place you shall hear ..."

> "... brought into an AMALGAMA (amalgam) of Mercury and of Sulphur, which presently seizes on him, corrodes all his members, and is dissolved, and is presently mortified of his Salt-water, into a most splendent transparent oil. You must note,

that this dissolution is not sufficient, and the King is not minded as yet to let go his Soul out of his fixed body, which you can see when you separate the water from the dissolved body of the King, where you shall find fixed powder of Gold, out of which you will hardly get his Soul that is therein."

"Therefore follow my counsel and bear the yoke, which I bore before you, and learn to know exactly in pains taking, further thus, as I shall inform you. Having dissolved your Gold wholly in the said water, and brought it into a pleasant yellow oil, then let it stand well luted for a day and a night in a very gentle BALNEUM MARIA (Bath of Maria), the FECES (faeces) which are settled, must be separated from it, then take this pure dissolution, put it into a well coated body, or Retort, apply a Helmet to it, with a Receiver, in the best manner luted to it, set it into a Sand Cupel (sand bath), drive the Gold with the water over the Helmet, iterate this a third time, abstract the water in BALNEUM MARIE, you will find a fair Gold powder, keep this in a glass for an hour in fire, let the remaining humidity be drawn from it."

It is the time to speak to you of the *Serpent* and of the *Eagle*, which is to say of the nitre and of the ammonium salt. All the salts used in alchemy, as we have already said, should be, so much as possible, of natural origin.

Nitre is a potassium salt well known at present as potassium nitrate and, anciently, as saltpetre, a name composed of the words salt and lithos, that is, 'stone salt.' In 'The Great Alchemical Work of Eirenaeus Philalethes and Nicholas Flamel' we already referred to its canonical preparation, therefore it isn't necessary to repeat it here.

The salt called ammonium chloride is the ammonium combination known anciently. It is a natural product of volcanic eruption and collects sublimated in the rifts of the rocks and in the caves of active volcanoes. The caravans of the East brought it, by the name of *salt of tartaria*, from central Asia.

In ancient times the trade in this salt destined for Europe was provisioned from Egypt, from the district of Ammonia, in Libya; from there came naturally the name that it still bears today.

In Egypt, and more particularly in Libya, it is found in the places where the caravans rested and where the camels urinated on the sand. The Sun's heat sublimated the salt onto the sand's surface.

Also, from the combustion of dry camel manure is formed the ammonium salt that is deposited with the soot in chimneys, from where it was extracted by *sublimation*.

Presently, it is very difficult, or maybe entirely impossible, to find it as it comes from its natural environment; therefore, you will have to prepare it yourself.

Acquire 1 kilogram of ammonium sulphate, often used as chemical fertiliser in the agricultural field, and also the same amount of common salt (sodium chloride) extracted directly from a saltpan.

Pour into a stainless steel container 3 litres of rainwater and heat it on a gas stove, at 40 degrees Celsius. Dissolve in the water the ammonium sulfate, stirring it with a wooden spoon, until all the salt is dissolved.

Then add, little by little, the common salt, dissolving it also in water. If you don't manage to dissolve all the salt, add more water, until it is completely dissolved. It is apparent that we can verify a chemical reaction here.

The ammonium sulphate, reacting with the chloride, combines with the sodium's chlorine to become ammonium chloride, and loses its sulfate to the sodium.

The salts resulting from this chemical reaction are sodium sulphate and the ammonium chloride, which crystallise at different temperatures. The sulphate crystallises first on the liquid's surface, in fine sheets like ice, or in the bottom of the container as hail. The chloride crystallises in flakes just like snow, which, with some experience, you will be able to easily separate through successive crystallisations.

Put together all of your chloride into a container, as you collect it, then dissolve it again in more rainwater. Crystallise it several times, until you obtain a salt as white as snowflakes, taking the precaution, during each crystallisation, to remove any sulphate that may be still forming.

From this method you will obtain a canonical salt, because the primary element acting in this chemical reaction is the chlorine freed by the natural sodium chloride.

We said that other less dangerous methods exist to obtain the canonical *Royal Water*; therefore we will describe another simpler method of preparing it.

To prepare this water you will need *ammonium salt* and *spirit of nitre*. We have already mentioned, and are never tired of repeating, that all salts and spirits used in alchemy must be canonical or philosophical; that is, of natural origin. It would be very easy to acquire the salts and the acids (spirits) in a warehouse for industrial chemical products or laboratory materials, but these, according to the Masters' teachings, are inappropriate for our Work, serving, only, for experimentation.

To prepare the nitre spirit canonically, it is necessary to distill in a good Pyrex glass alembic, or better, in a sandstone one, on a gas stove, with controlled temperature and in a sand bath, a mixture of 2 pounds of Mars or Venus *vitriol*, and 1 pound of thin powdered nitre.

Natural vitriol is an iron or copper *sulphate*, or a mixture of both, that can be extracted for crystallisation from the water of the small artificial lakes that are formed on the ground in pyrite or chalcopyrite mines, that form through rainwater infiltrating such mines.

After having crystallised it, the vitriol will have to be dried in the sunlight or *calcined*, to extract its superfluous humidity – only then can it be used. Further on we will see why, as we prepare the canonical vitriol.

After having poured the materials into the alembic, begin the *distillation* with a soft fire to extract the phlegm, and, only then, increase the temperature until the spirit begins to distill, as will be observed from the glittering vapours (reddish) that fill the cucurbit completely, helmet and the container.

After all the spirit has passed into the container, cease the fire, to let the cucurbit cool and so that you may remove from it the faeces, using a long handled wooden spoon. Repeat the same operation in order to obtain about 1 litre of spirit. Rectify it, until you obtain a strong spirit of more than 30 degrees Baume. The alembic will constitute a 3 litre cucurbit and a 1.5 litre helmet with an IN55 male joint and a 2 litre receiving flask with an air hole. Grease all the joints with silicon.

To prepare the *Royal Water*, pour into a 1 litre Pyrex spherical glass matrass (balloon) spirit of nitre and heat it up to 30 degrees Celsius, in an electric or gas stove with controlled temperature in a sand bath. After warming it, place it in a well ventilated situation so that the vapours escape freely into the outside air. Then pour in, little by little, successively, 60 grams of ammonium salt. The chemical reaction won't begin immediately but, as soon as it begins, it is uncontrollable.

It is best that the spirit of nitre doesn't fill more than ¼ of the capacity of the volume of the flask, otherwise it would overflow, during the reaction, and spilling the corrosive acid out of the flask could cause serious burns. The reaction is accompanied by a great gaseous emanation, the reason for which this operation should be only carried out in a well-ventilated place, preferably outdoors, as we already explained to you.

After the chemical reaction is finished and the ammonium salt has been all dissolved and cannot to be dissolved further, the water you now have will be a beautiful yellow colour. Let it cool and keep it in a glass flask with a ground glass stopper.

Here we have it then, Brothers, the method by which the canonical salts are manufactured, as well as the spirit of nitre and the *Royal Water*. We have explained to you in few lines that which we have taken years to learn.

Follow to-the-letter all of the instructions and you will be gratified. It is natural that you won't succeed the first time carrying out the processes just as you have been shown. However, with practice, you will reach your goal, just as we did, and as other Brothers have also.

THE THIRD KEY

A winged dragon with coiled tail and pointed tongue stands in a landscape with high mountains in the background. On the left behind the dragon, a wolf or fox, runs off holding a bird (possibly a hen) in its mouth and is attacked by a cockerel riding on its back.

Canseliet's comment to the Third Key in the French edition:

> "The dragon is the origin of the two natures, aqueous and igneous and it is the basis of the combat, wherein they surrender, he occupies the subject of the whole first plan of this composition. Of him is born directly the fox chosen by Basil Valentine, in a physical analogy that underlines, according to us, this curious fact that the name of the astute quadruped is of the feminine kind in all the Aryan languages."

In the text of the Third Key we see the following, essentially:

> "But no such triumph can take place unless the King imparts great strength and potency to his water and tinges it with his own colour, that thereby he may be consumed and become invisible, and then again recover his visible form, with a diminution of his simple essence, and a development of his perfection."

> "This Tincture is the Rose of our Masters, of purple hue, called also the red blood of the Dragon ..."

Let us now see the text of the Third Key, just as it is described in *The Last Will and Testament*:

§§ CLEF.III.

The Third Key of Basil Valentine: Above, engraving from Michael Maier's *Tripus aureus* (1618), and below, earlier reversed variant.

"Then take of good spirit of Salt-niter one part, and of dephlegmed Spirit of ordinary salt, three parts, pour these spirits together warmed a little, into a body on the fore-written Gold powder, lute a Helmet and Receiver to it, drive the Gold over as formerly in sand several times with an iterated distillation, the oftner the better, let the Gold come to be volatile more and more, and at last let all come over. By this repeated driving over, its fixed body is divided, all its members are torn asunder, and opened, and leaves willingly its Soul to a Special judge, of which my third Key will give sufficient information."

"Note further, that after this work those salt spirits must be abstracted from the Gold, which was driven over, very gently in BALNEO MARIE, let nothing of the tincture of the Gold come over, that the body suffer not any diminution; then take that Gold, or rather these Crystals of Gold from which you have separated the water, put it in a reverberating pan, set it under a mussle, let its first fire be gentle for an hour, when all its corrosiveness be taken away, then your powder will be of a fair scarlet colour, as subtle as ever was seen, put it in a clean viol, pour on it fresh spirit of ordinary salt, first brought to a sweetness, let it stand in a gentle digestion, let that spirit be deeply tinged and transparent, red like a Ruby, cant off, pour on fresh, extract again, iterate the work of canting off and pouring on, till no more tincture of it appears, put all these extractions together, separate them in BALNEG (bath) gently from the Sulphur of SOL, then that powder is subtle and tender; of great worth; this matter is such, which in a short process transmutes LUNA in its tincture to the highest perfection, according to the direction of my XII Keys."

"He that has some knowledge herein, may make this quire; whither this extracted dry Soul and Sulphur of the King be just that Soul, of which Philosophers have this saying ..."

What can we understand, then, about that which the Master tells us in these Three Keys?

In the First, he teaches us to purify the gold, or the Sun, with the antimony; in the Second, the preparation of the *Royal Water* for the King's bath is described with view to its dissolution and, in the Third, the extraction of alchemical Sulphur from gold.

If you are well familiar with the text of the Third Key, you will notice the Master recommends dissolving the gold in a *Royal Water* composed of three parts of spirit of salt, and one part of spirit of nitre.

We have already said that we should prepare this *Royal Water* with spirit of nitre and with ammonium salt. To prepare the water described by the Master, in the Third Key, you will need the spirit of common salt, of which is said still nothing.

The canonical spirit of common salt, that is muriatic or hydrochloric acid, is extracted, obviously, from common salt extracted from the sea salt pan. The first operation in this process is to execute the salt's *calcination*, that is, its decrepitation.

Put 250 grams of rough salt extracted directly from sea salt pan, in a big iron frying pan or an enameled iron pan, and place on a close-fitting cover, because, if it is not close fitting, the salt will jump out when it crackles.

Place the frying pan with the salt on a gas stove, with strong fire. After some time, the salt will begin to crackle. As soon as it stops crackling, remove the cover and, with a stainless steel spoon, mix the salt so that it *calcines* completely. Repeat the operation until the salt stops crackling completely. Let it cool a little and pour it, by successive fractions, into a big porcelain or Pyrex glass mortar, and grind it well, until it is all reduced to fine powder, the finer the better. Repeat the process until you have obtained 1-2 kilograms of powdered salt.

You will now need an alembic like that which was used to distill the spirit of nitre.

Put in a ceramic dish 2 pounds of vitriol, well warmed by the Sun or *calcined* to a whiteness, reduced to fine powder, and 1 pound of common salt well decrepited (dessicated), also reduced to very fine powder.

Mix the two salts intimately, with a spoon, and then pour them into a 3 litre cucurbit. Place the cucurbit on a gas stove into a dish and sand bath. Introduce the helm and affix to it the receiver – ensure that this has an air hole, and grease all joints with silicon.

At the beginning keep a gentle fire in order to exude the matter and, afterwards, increase the heat gradually so that the spirits distill.

When everything has distilled, turn off the fire and let the alembic cool. Remove the faeces from the cucurbit with a long handled wooden spoon and then repeat the process until you obtain at least 1 litre of spirit.

Rectify it as the Art demands, to 30 degrees Baume or more. Keep it in a flask with a ground glass stopper. It is this canonical spirit of salt that you will use, together with the spirit of nitre, to prepare this last *Royal Water*.

To satisfy your curiosity we can tell you that, at present, this *Royal Water* is still prepared with the same proportions of these two spirits: three parts of spirit of salt or muriatic acid, and one part of spirit of nitre or azotic acid. This confirms Master Basil Valentine's great knowledge, and our suggestion of his being the greatest alchemist and spagyrist of all time.

Also, in the Third Key there is reference to the *sweetened spirit of salt*. This spirit has for its purpose the dissolution of the *calcined* salt of gold and to reduce it to very subtle powder, of a purple colour, with a view to the extraction of its alchemical Sulphur.

This spirit has characteristics similar to actual hydrochloric ether and its preparation is described in the practical techniques to which the Master refers us in *The Last Will and Testament*:

> "Note, that without information you cannot attain unto the Spirit of Salt, if it be not sweet, it has no extractive power; to the attaining hereof, observe these following manuals; take good Spirit of Salt, dephlegmed exactly, driven forth, in that manner, as you shall hear anon."

> "Take one part of it, add half a part to it of the best Spirit of wine, which must not have any phlegm, but must be a mere Sulphur of wine, and must be prepared in that manner, as I shall tell you anon; lute a helmet to it, draw it over strongly, leave nothing behind; to the abstracted put more Spirit of wine, draw it over, somewhat stronger than you did the first time, weigh it, put a third time more to it, draw it over again, well luted, putrefy this for half a month, or so long as it be sweet, and it is done in Balney (bath) very gently; thus the Spirit of wine and Salt is prepared, lost it corrosiveness, and is fit for extracting."

In this Key, the pictorial representation agrees with the description in the text, because the *Sulphur* of gold, before its fixation, was volatile, it having gone through the beak of the alembic with its respective water. Thus the winged Dragon represents, and very accurately, the volatile and the fixed.

Alchemicaly, three very well known principles constitute the Philosopher's Stone or *Universal Medicine*: *Sulphur, Mercury* and *Salt*.

Previously we explained the alchemical meaning of these three principles. These can be extracted from different materials, and then, combined together in their proper proportions, in the final cooking flask.

At the end of the operations described in the Third Key we have obtained, just, a subtle powder, dry and incombustible, of the colour purple, which is, as we previously said, the Sulphur of gold. We lack, at this point, therefore, two more principles: the Mercury and the Salt. To extract from this gold these two further principles it would be necessary to obtain a great amount of vitriol (Salt) of gold, which would be impractical, given the high price of this noble metal.

Therefore, the Master says in *The Last Will and Testament*:

> "In Gold there is no waterish humidity at all, unless it were reduced again into Vitriol, which would be but an useless and unprofitable work, and would require huge expenses, in case the Philosopher's Stone should be of Vitriol of Gold, of which there must be had great store ..."

> "But what Countries, Goods, Lands, have been dilapidated this way, I wave to discourse of only, this warning I give to my Disciples, nature having left a nearer way to keep and to imitate that, that they also might take heed to fall into such extreme and inextricable poverty."

It is evident that this process is against nature and could induce his disciples to an extreme poverty, as the Master charitably affirms. Therefore, it concludes the explanation of the text of the *Twelve Keys*, to indicate the method of the extraction of the three principles from *Roman vitriol*.

> "But remember well that these Mineral Spirits are in other Metals also, and are found effectual in one Mineral, from whence with more ease and less charges it may be had; the business is only herein, that you learn to know, what this Mercurial Spirit, Mercurial Soul, and Astral Salt is, that the one may

not be taken in stead of the other, which would cause a huge error."

"...therefore the ASTRUM of SOL (Sol star, or Sulphur) is found not only in Gold, that with the addition of the Spirit of Mercury and the SOLAR Salt only the Philosopher's Stone could be made, but may in like manner, be prepared artificially out of Copper and Steel, two immature Metals, both which as male and female have red tinging qualities, as well as Gold itself, whither the same be taken out of one alone, or out of both, being first entered into an union."

"To be further as good as I promised, concerning other things, quoted in my KEYS, know ye, that no Philosopher is tied wholly unto the Metal of Gold, of which I spoke largely hitherto, and described the true fundamentals thereof ..."

"Such Souls and goldish SULPHURS are found most effectual in MARS and VENUS, as also in VITRIOL, and both VENUS and MARS can be reduced into a most effectual VITRIOL, in which Metalline VITRIOL afterward all the three PRINCIPLES as MERCURY, SULPHUR, and SALT are found under one heaven, and with little pains and short time each can be taken out of it apart, as you shall hear, when I shall make further relation of the Mineral VITRIOL, which is dug in HUNGARY, of a high gradation."

Basil Valentine directs us towards a canonical native vitriol of Mars and Venus (see Plate II-h), obtained from Hungary, which one can also find, with relative ease, in Portugal, in its small lakes, near the pyrite and chalcopyrite mines. In this natural vitriol we also find these three principles.

"However none is thus much dignified in its worthiness, that the said Philosophic Stone could be made of it as this VITRIOL is. There ancient Philosophers have concealed this Mineral as much as ever they could, and would not reveal the same to their own children, that they should not divulge it in the world, but be kept SECRET, though they published, that such preparation is made out of one thing, and out of one body, which has the nature of SOL and LUNA, and contains also the Mercury, wherein they said true enough because it is so."

"For the best, which according to my experience showed itself most effectual, herein is that, which is broken, and dug in HUNGARY, of a very deep degree of tincture, not very unlike unto fair blue SAPPHIRE, having very little of humidities, and other additional, or strange ores; the oftener it is dissolved and coagulated, the more is it exalted in its deep tingeing colour, and is beheld with great admiration."

"This high graduated VITRIOL is found crude in those places, where Gold, Copper, Iron, is broken and dug, and is abundantly transported from thence into foreign parts, insomuch that sometimes there is great scantiness of it in those parts, and elsewhere."

It is the occasion, now, for us to speak to you about this canonical vitriol that the Master says we may find in Hungary. We mentioned previously and we shall once again, that a natural vitriol with these characteristics one can obtain, with ease, in Portugal.

As we have said, near pyrite and chalcopyrite mines, upon the ground, are formed small lakes whose water came from the filtration of rainwater into the mines, which bring, together, in

PLATE III

The First Key of Basil Valentine: Crude woodcut from the second edition of the *Twelve Keys* (Zerbst, 1602). Image courtesy of Adam McLean.

PLATE IV

The Second Key of Basil Valentine: Crude woodcut from the second edition of the *Twelve Keys* (Zerbst, 1602). Image courtesy of Adam McLean.

PLATE V

The Third Key of Basil Valentine: Crude woodcut from the second edition of the *Twelve Keys* (Zerbst, 1602). Image courtesy of Adam McLean.

PLATE VI

Two versions of the twelfth image from Basil Valentine's *Azoth* series, first published in
Azoth, ou Le moyen de faire l'or caché des Philosophes (Paris, 1659), and said to illustrate
the seven alchemical operations in their correct order: Above, from the original, and
below, hand-coloured version by Adam McLean.

dissolution, the salts of Mars and Venus. In the summer these waters evaporate, leaving large amounts of crystallised vitriol. Also inside the mines some amount of very pure crystallised salt exists, in pendants as stalactites that can weigh some many kilos.

Vitriol in this state of purity is difficult to get. However, the other salt that crystallises outside the mines, is relatively easily collected, but is quite impure.

To purify it, acquire a dozen or so kilos of the best salts available. Heat it up to 60 degrees Celsius, in a stainless steel container, in 25 litres of rainwater. After having brought the heat up to this temperature, regulate the fire and pour, little by little, the salt into the water, and as this is dissolving, keep it moving with a long handled wooden spoon.

When the solution is saturated, that is, when the salt no longer dissolves at 60 degrees Celsius, filter the hot liquid by a funnel with a very clean linen cloth, into another similar container. Leave it to rest for one night.

The following day you will find, in the container, the salt crystallised into very pure beautiful blue-green crystals. Retrieve them with a wooden spoon, carefully. If any are stuck to the bottom of the container, remove them with a wooden spatula. Usually, under the crystals appears a moist iron oxide of ochre colour. If this happens, wash it out in the *Mother Water*, to separate the oxide, and place it, clean, on a cotton cloth to evaporate, sheltered out of direct sunlight.

Filter the liquid again and heat it up to evaporate the excess water, reducing it to a third of its volume. Let it crystallise, as previously, and repeat the process until you can drain off all the *Mother Water*.

By this method you will obtain an excellent canonical vitriol that will allow you to extract the three principles referred to by the Master in *The Last Will and Testament*.

For this extraction you will need a suitable alembic, manufactured in refractory ceramic or sandstone. Pyrex glass doesn't tolerate the necessary temperature, required for the vitriol's *distillation*, without breaking. As it will be near impossible for you to find this kind of alembic at a specialist suppliers, you will have to order it from an expert potter.

The cucurbit of the aforesaid alembic should have, at least, a capacity of 5-10 litres, and a 3 litre helmet. We can also use a Glauber retort made of the same material.

Before the *distillation* of the vitriol, it is necessary to proceed to its *rubification* or *calcination*.

But first let us return to the text of *The Last Will and Testament*, to see, as the Master teaches, the *distillation* of vitriol:

> "If you get such deep graduated and well prepared Mineral, called VITRIOL, then pray to God for understanding and wisdom for your intention and after you have calcined it, put it into a well coated Retort, drive it gently at first, then increase the fire, there comes in the form of a white Spirit of Vitriol in the manner of a horrid fume, or wind, and comes into the Receiver as long as it has any such material in it. And now, that in this wind are invisibly hid all the THREE PRINCIPLES, and come together out of that dwelling, therefore it is not necessary, to seek and search always in precious things, because by this means there is a nearer way open unto natures mysteries, and is held forth to all such; which are able to conceive of Art and Wisdom."

> "Now if you separate and free this expelled spirit well and purely PER MODUM DISTILLATIONIS (by *distillations*), from its earthly humidity, then in the bottom of the glass you will find the treasure, and fundamentals of all the Philosophers, and yet known to few, which is a red oil, as ponderous in weight as ever any Lead, or Gold may be, as thick as blood, of a burning fiery quality, which is that true fluid Gold of the Philosophers, which nature drove together

from the three principles, where in is found a Spirit, Soul, and Body, and is that PHILOSOPHIC GOLD, saving one, which is its dissolution, during the fire, and not subject to any corruptibleness, else it flies away with Body and Soul, for neither water nor earth can do it any hurt, because it receives its first birth and beginning from a heavenly water, which in due time is poured down upon the earth."

"In these together driven goldish waters lie hid that true bird and EAGLE, the King with his heavenly SPLENDOUR together with its clarified SALT, which three you find shut up in this one thing and golden property, and from thence you will get all that, which you have need of for your intention."

As the Master says, in the *distillation* of the Hungarian vitriol, first is produced, violently, a white spirit, and then a red oil. This *distillation* is carried out, as previously mentioned, with very strong fire in an alembic or Glauber retort.

To condense the spirits, you will need a large Pyrex glass receiver cooled with very cold water, or a cooling mixture of common salt and ice.

When the last red drops stop coming over, remove the receiver and pour the fetid spirit into a tightly sealed glass jar closed with a ground glass stopper.

This spirit is the Philosopher's Chaos, where are contained the three principles that it is necessary to separate by *distillation*.

The *Mercurial Spirit* – separate from the Chaos by *distillation* and afterwards rectify as the Art demands, it should be limpid and as transparent as crystal. It is through this spirit that the *Sulphur* and the Philosopher's *Salt* will be extracted from the caput mortem that remains in the cucurbit of the alembic after the *distillation* of the *Mercurial Spirit*.

"For if you can separate this Spirit of Vitriol, as it ought, then that affords again unto you three principles, out of which only, without a either addition, from the beginning of the world the Philosopher's Stone has been made from that, you have to expect again a Spirit of a white form, an oil of red quality, after these two a Crystalline Salt, these three being duly joined in their perfection, generate no less than the Philosopher's great Stone; for that white Spirit is merely the Philosopher's Mercury, the red oil is the Soul, and the Salt is that true Magnetic body, as I told you formerly."

"... after the Spirit is separated from it, then the Salt appears in its purity; if that process be further followed, and after a true order and measure the conjunction be undertaken, and the Spirit and Salt be set together into the Philosophic furnace, then it appears again, how the heavenly Spirit strives in a Magnetic way to attract its own Salt, it dissolves the same within XL (40) days, bringing it to an uniform water with itself, even as the Salt has been before its coagulation. In that destruction and dissolution appears the hugest blackness an ECLIPSE, and darkness of the earth, that ever was seen. But in the exchange thereof a bright glittering whiteness appearing, then the case is altered, and the dissolved fluid waterish Salt turns into a Magnet; for in that dissolution it lays hold on its own Spirit, which is the Spirit of Mercury, attracting the same powerfully like a Magnet, hiding it under a form of a dry clear body, bringing the same by way of uniting into a deep coagulation and firm fixedness by means of a continued fire, and the certain degrees thereof."

"Thus in brief you have a short relation of Vitriol, Sulphur, and Magnet. Pray to God for grace, that you may conceive right of it, put it then to good use, and be mindful of the poor and needy."

"Oh! Good God, what do these ignorant men think, is not this a very easy and child-like labour? The one begets the other, and the one comes from the other, is there not bread baked of corn, upon distinct works? But the World is blind, and will be so to the end of it; thus much at this time, and I commit thee to the protection of the Highest."

Here, Basil Valentine finishes the third part of his book, *The Last Will and Testament*, in what refers to the work with vitriol.

The Fourth Key represents the *putrefaction* followed by the *albification*. By increasing the degree of the fire we will have the regimes of *Venus, Mars* and, finally that of the *Sun*.

The *multiplication* will find its place then in the dissolution of the red stone in Mercury or the *Mercurial Spirit*, and re-digesting, again passing through all the regimes and, by this path, successively passing to the third *multiplication*.

In the last key, given in plain language, the Master teaches us how a *transmutation* is performed.

In Basil Valentine's *Twelve Keys*, as we have seen, his work begins with the *purification* of the common gold by means of antimony with a view to the extraction of its Philosophical Sulphur. A person not having read *The Last Will and Testament*, would, we perceive, come across a difficulty which would suggest that he may abandon the actual way for one which is impractical, that is – he would probably follow the vitriol path.

For that reason, in our understanding, only few alchemists will come to understand the text of *Twelve Keys* without having read, first, *The Last Will and Testament*.

THE GREAT ALCHEMICAL WORK OF

Basil Valentine: Part Two

VEGETABLE AND MINERAL SPAGYRICS

B asil Valentine, as we said, was one of the greatest alchemists and spagyricists of all time, and this is very evident from his books *Revelation of the Mysteries of the Tinctures of the Seven Metals* and *The Triumphal Chariot of Antimony*.

We won't describe the 'receipts' of the Master, because they are not easily executed by most of the Art's Brothers. However, we will try to describe another much simpler method and practice that will aid you in gaining skill in manual techniques.

In vegetable and mineral spagyrics there are two very important and indispensable spirits: they are the spirits of wine, and of vinegar.

SPIRIT OF WINE

To distill the spirit of wine you will need an alembic of good Pyrex glass which has a 6 litre cucurbit with a flat bottom, a 2 litre helmet with a ground glass IN70 throat and a ground glass beak of IN19.

The receiver should be a 2 litre bowl with a flat bottom, and a ground glass joint of IN29. Between the helmet beak and the receiver you should have a joint of IN19/29 with an air hole. Also you will need a gas or electric stove with controlled temperature (see Plate II-1) and a sand bath.

To begin the practical work, acquire at least 50 litres of good red wine at 11 or 12 degrees alcohol.

Pour 5 litres of wine into the cucurbit, connect the helmet and the receiver and grease their joints. Leave the whole for some time in digestion on gentle fire, at a temperature of 40 degrees Celsius, then distill at 80 degrees Celsius (maximum).

When you have distilled 1 litre over into the receiver, stop the *distillation* and discard the phlegm that is in the cucurbit. From the faeces of this phlegm you can, then, extract a salt as we will explain to you further on, when we speak of the extraction of the spirit of the vinegar.

Your distilled spirit will be approximately 45 percent alcohol on the first *distillation*. Pour it into a large glass bottle and close it well.

In the same way, distill the remaining 45 litres of wine and join all the distilled spirits together. When all the wine is distilled you will have 10 litres of spirit at 45 percent purity measured on the alcohol meter.

Wash the cucurbit and pour into it 5 litres of spirit at 45 percent. Replace the helmet and the receiver, and, as before, distil again at

80 degrees Celsius. When you have distilled 2 litres of the spirit, stop the *distillation*. The spirit in the receiver will be at least 90 percent. Distil what remains of the 5 litres as previously. Add this spirit to the other of the same graduation.

Now, apply a 40 centimetre length attachment to the throat of your alembic and replace the helmet there. This increase in length will hinder the rise of water into the helmet and will allow you, in this way, to collect a stronger distilled spirit.

Pour 4 litres of the 90 percent spirit into the cucurbit and add to it 10 percent of its volume (40 grams) of recently dried (quick) lime. Replace the helmet and the receiver and distill at the temperature of 78 degrees Celsius until there only just passes into the receiver 2 litres of spirit. Pour that spirit into a large glass bottle, close well, and continue the *distillation* into the receiver another 1.8 litres or less. Now stop the *distillation*.

If you proceed to-the-letter with what we have described to you, you will have distilled a spirit of wine with a very close graduation of nearly 100 percent purity measured in the alcohol meter, at the temperature of 15 degrees Celsius.

If you don't manage this the first time, repeat the last phase and distill a little less spirit over into the receiver.

Keep it in a glass bottle, very tightly sealed, to avoid the aerial humidity adulterating it.

This canonical spirit of wine will be very useful in all the spagyrical operations, mainly in the preparation of the sweetened spirit of salt and, in a similar manner, in the preparation of vegetable and metallic tinctures.

SPIRIT OF VINEGAR

Acquire at least 50 litres of good pure vinegar of red wine at 10 percent acid. Reject industrial vinegar because it is manufactured with the use of chemical products.

Acquire four 1.5 litre plastic bottles like, for example, the bottles that soda drinks come in.

Pour the vinegar into the bottles, without filling them completely, leaving, at least, the space of three fingers, empty.

Place the bottles in a freezer, with the bottles standing upright, so that the liquid doesn't get to the lids of the bottles.

Leave long enough to freeze the vinegar well. When everything is frozen, remove the lid and place the bottle mouth down into a large-mouthed 1 litre glass flask. Let it drain its half litre of vinegar into the flask. Then change the bottle for the next one and an empty flask, so that it drains another half litre. There will be remaining in the plastic bottles a discoloured ice that contains only water. The first vinegar that is collected is slippery and will have roughly a 4 degrees Baume. That which remains will have about 2 degrees.

Add together, in a large 5 litre plastic bottle, all the vinegar of the same graduation. Repeat the same process with all the vinegar you have.

Fill now the bottles with the less graduated vinegar and proceed in the same way, freezing as previously, to obtain the vinegar of 4 degrees Baume. Join it to the other collection of the same graduation. Fill, again, the bottles with this further graduated vinegar. Repeat each time the same process until you obtain, by freezing the vinegar, at least 8 to 9 degrees.

When you have all the vinegar with this level, proceed to its *distillation*. For the process you will require an alembic and the same stove as was used to distill the spirit of wine.

Pour in the cucurbit 5 litres of vinegar. Distil to gentle fire about 2.5 litres, and the remainder to strong fire. The first spirit to leave is a spirit of a beautiful lemon colour and it will have just 1 or 2 degrees Baume. The remainder will be more graduated. What remains in the bottom of the cucurbit is a liquid as thick as honey that you will keep in a separate container.

Pour the various graduations of the distilled spirit into separate sealed containers.

Pour in the cucurbit another 5 litres of vinegar and repeat the previous process until you have distilled all your vinegar provision.

Fill the bottles with the distilled spirit again and freeze, as previously, always separating the spirit of different graduations. By freezing the distilled vinegar it will be very difficult to get better than 5 or 6 degrees. When you have the spirit at 5 or 6 degrees Baume, pour it into the cucurbit, after you have washed it very well with a solution of sodium hydroxide, and distil the vinegar in the same way, starting with a weak heat in the beginning.

The spirit that comes over first is always the weakest, and that which remains in the cucurbit will approach close to 9 or 10 degrees Baume. Repeat the process until you have all your spirit to 10 degrees. With this level the spirit of vinegar will contain more than 80 percent of natural acetic acid, and it will dissolve any metallic calx. To the touch it is greasy like oil of tartar.

In relationship to the 'honey' that remained after the vinegar *distillation*, pour it into the cucurbit and distil it at very strong heat. A highly graduated spirit will come over that you should add to the other you prepared. Remaining in the bottom of the cucurbit you will see the faeces that you should remove and *calcine* in a stainless steel or ceramic dish with a very strong fire, on a gas stove. After it is well *calcined*, leach the remains with rainwater and coagulate the salt as the Art demands.

After being coagulated and dried this salt is very deliquescent.

This is a true salt tartar that will be useful to you in several spagyrical preparations.

DISTILLED VEGETABLES

The *distillation* of vegetable matter will only be possible with plants that contain essential oils.

Pick, at a suitable time, the flowering blooms of the plants that you desire to work with and that have plenty of essential oil. Cut them into the small pieces and fill the cucurbit of an alembic with them, like the one used to distill the spirit of wine and of vinegar. Pour in 500 millilitres of spirit of wine, rectified, and 250 millilitres of rainwater or dew.

Distill, first, with very gentle heat, afterwards stronger, so that it distills all of the spirit of wine. Repeat three times this same operation, always distilling the same spirit that you have introduced into the cucurbit. The distillate will be a little more than just spirit of wine because it will draw together, with it, water and the essential oil of the plant that will be soluble in the spirit of wine.

After everything has distilled over, extinguish the fire and let all cool. Remove the helmet, and with a strong wire hook remove all the plant material and dry it in the sun.

After everything is completely dry, incinerate on a tin foil sheet. Collect the ashes and place them in an iron frying (or enameled) pan, on a gas stove.

Calcine them with a very strong fire; mix well with a stainless steel spoon, until everything is well *calcined* and of a uniform grey colour.

Pour into a 1 litre wide-mouthed glass flask 0.5 litres of rainwater or distilled dew and then pour in, by successive fractions, the aforementioned ashes while still hot. Then leave to rest.

In a glass flask, like the previous one, place a glass funnel, with a cotton lid and filter.

If the ashes were well *calcined*, as the Art demands, the water will be clear and transparent, otherwise it will be of a tea colour.

That filtered water will be poured into a porcelain container and placed on a gas stove in a sand bath, in order to coagulate the salt. Towards the end of the coagulation, the thickened liquid will produce a thin film on its surface that impedes evaporation. When the solution arrives at this point we recommend that you stir the liquid, with a glass rod, to break up the thin surface layer. The coagulated salt (crystallised) should be as white as snow. If it isn't, it is because you have not *calcined* the ashes properly; you will have to re-*calcine* the salt and repeat the same operation until it is as white as snow.

Pour the salt hot into your distillate and shake circularly so that it is more easily dissolved. Let it rest and to circulate in a pelican, made of a 1 litre matrass with another joined to it, above, of 250 millilitre volume, connected by a IN29 ground glass joint.

The water contained in the spirit of wine usually dissolves the salt. If it is not dissolved completely, the excess will crystallise in the matrass bottom.

This is a process of vegetable medicine which is a little rough, but superior to the common types of tincture, for we have incorporated the salt of the plant with all its oligoelements.

VEGETABLE PRIMUM ENS AND SALT VOLATILISATION

"If you are not able to obtain the Alkahest you might learn, at least, how to volatilise the salt of tartar ..." (Van Helmont).

The volatilisation of the salt of tartar is one of the great vegetable arcana of our Art, and only a few alchemists know how it is achieved. So, we will try to transmit to you this arcana, limiting our explanation only by the conditions that the Tradition forces upon us.

The volatilised salt of tartar is a great medicine, as the old iatrochemists affirm. By them the method of tartar's volatilisation has always been a jealously kept secret.

"This salt, says Van Helmont, a famous medical iatrochemist, is converted by alchemy, being volatilised, equals in virtue most other secrets for its nature is resolutive and detergent and, in this way, it can penetrate into the human body to the fourth digestion, dissolving and causing to pass the excrementitious humours and the coagulations against-nature that meet in the organs. This salt carries away with it all residues that meet in the veins, it dissolves the most obstinate obstructions, dissipating, in this way, the material cause of the diseases."

In modern terminology this salt is a powerful solvent of the urates. Medical iatrochemists treated with success the calculus and other similar afflictions, almost exclusively with volatilised salt of tartar.

A great contemporary spagyricist, Alexander Von Bernus, author of the book *Alchemie et medicine*, who prepared in his laboratory, Soluna, in Germany, biochemical salts distilled or spagyrically volatilised, lost a judicial battle against a competitor, because the specialists of conventional science – chemists – insisted that these salts could not be distilled, that is, volatilised. Von Bernus preferred to lose the case rather than have to disclose the secret of this process.

Volatilise the fixed salt of a plant (potassium carbonate) and get it to pass through the throat and beak of a retort? "Never!" the adherents of conventional science will say. However, for the pleasure of our eyes and thanks to our Art, the salt flows volatilised, through the beak of the retort, transparent as ice, slipping into the receiver.

It is known that four elements exist in the nature: *Air, Fire, Earth* and *Water*. Of these four elements, two are kindred and the other two are contrary. The oil, or the essential oil and the water, are contrary elements. If you will pour water into hot oil, the oil repels the water violently.

The *Vegetable Primum Ens* is the intimate union of the three principles, *Sulfur* (essential oil), *Mercury* (alcohol) and *Salt* (potassium carbonate).

There are two ways to volatilise this salt: a long and slow way, and another shorter way. The first was transmitted to us through the charity of a Brother of the Art, and the other faster and expedite method was discovered by ourselves.

Take at least 5-10 kilograms of 'fresh' rosemary (*Rosmarinus officinalis*) and dry it in the shade. After the plant is dry, incinerate it on tin foil or on a clean flagstone. Extract its salt as I explained in the previous operation.

Acquire from a specialist, or distill from the plant, 150 millilitres of essential oil of rosemary and pour it into a small 250 or 500 millilitre Pyrex glass retort. Place the retort into a small electric or gas stove with controlled temperature, in a sand bath with a 250 millilitre spherical receiver, with an air-hole.

Connect to the retort its receiver. Pour into the bowl of the retort, by successive fractions, 30 grams of the salt *treated*, as Art demands. A violent reaction will be produced and the essential oil will turn as dark as coffee.

Distil, allowing the essential oil to boil lightly. When most of the oil has passed into the receiver and there remains in the bottom of the retort a dark liquid as thick as honey, stop the *distillation* and let it cool.

Then, pour into the retort bowl the distilled oil. Repeat the process twice more and, on the third time, distill to the end with a stronger heat without boiling. You will see, rising, then, a white vapor that moves up from the faeces in the retort bottom and solidifies like ice in neck and in the beak of the retort.

Repeat this twice and distill until most of the salt has come over into the receiver. Pour, now, some essential oil into the retort, so that this, when distilling, pulls the salt that is still deposited in its throat and beak into the receiver.

Let everything cool and clean the faeces out with turpentine essence or another appropriate solvent. After the retort is again completely clean, pour into its bowl the essential oil with the incorporated salt.

Add to this the same amount a distillate of the flowers of the same plant macerated in spirit of wine, fully rectified (its Mercury), and near 100 percent pure. Distil at a gentle heat and, towards the end, a little stronger; then you will see flow the salt as previously, but this time much more limpid and crystalline.

After everything is distilled, clean the retort again and repeat in this way, successively, until there are no more faeces left in the bottom if the bowl.

If you want to separate the volatilised salt from the Sulphur and the Mercury, when the salt is all coagulated in the retort neck and beak (see Plate II-j), change of receiver, let everything cool and pour into the retort some spirit of wine near 100 percent pure. Distill. The spirit of wine will pull all the salt into the clean receiver. Pour this saturated spirit of salt into a porcelain container and leave it to evaporate slowly. The salt will remain in the bottom. Keep it in a very tightly closed glass flask, because it is volatile.

If you want to conserve, united, the three principles, pour the liquid of the *Vegetable Primum Ens* distilled – Sulphur, Mercury and Salt – into a glass flask closed tightly, sheltered from the light.

The *Primum Ens of Rosmarinus officinalis* acts on all of the diseases that this plant is traditionally attributed to, but it is much more effective than the simple essential oil, for it has incorporated into it its Mercury and its volatilised salt.

If you are sufficiently perspicacious you will discover in this text the key to this operation that we here have taught you in plain language, because we have left out a small operative detail without which it will be impossible to volatilise the salt and cannot be done by chance.

If you don't manage to find this key, we are sorry, but tradition imposes silence on us about this.

TINCTURE OF IRON OR OF MARS

To begin this process look for, in very old houses, or on rural properties, iron railings or gates, that with the elapse of many years have been oxidised and have rusty pieces (hydrated oxide), in thick layers, that easily peel off.

Collect that Mars oxide and grind it into a very thin powder in an iron mortar. After it is very finely powdered, sift it in a sieve of 120 lines per inch, or 60 per centimetre, and *calcine* it well in a ceramic or a stainless steel dish on a gas stove with very strong fire.

This hydrated iron oxide can also be obtained from martial pyrites dissolved in spirit of nitre, after being precipitated by potassium carbonate and, finally, *calcined* in a very strong fire.

Pour 50 grams of that natural Mars oxide *calcined* into a 1 litre glass Pyrex matrass or incubator, and pour in 500 millilitres of spirit of vinegar at pH 10.

Close the matrass with a flask of 150 millilitres and a ground glass male joint of IN29.

Place the matrass on a small electric oven with controlled temperature.

Digest at 40 degrees Celsius. Every day shake the matrass circularly so that the material that has settled down in the bottom unglues and can be dissolved more easily in the spirit of vinegar. After 10 days, the vinegar will be saturated with the Mars tincture, which is of a beautiful dark brown colour like coffee.

Uncover the matrass and pour, or decant, into another matrass, all of the tinctured spirit. Pour onto the remaining material the same amount of spirit and leave to digest for 10 more days. Remove, by decantation, the spirit, and add it to the previous.

Pour all the tinctured spirit into an alembic as we referred to previously. Distil with a strong heat, to remove the vinegar spirit, which, after having distilled, will be useful for another operation or, otherwise, add it to another batch of the same graduation.

Don't distill to dryness, because you will run the risk of oxidising your salt. Leave, at least, in the bottom of the cucurbit, 100 millilitres of liquid. Leave to cool. On the following day you will find in the cucurbit a Martial Salt (acetate) crystallised in layers.

Pour off the liquid, by decantation, and remove the Salt. Place it inside a porcelain container, in an evaporating heat that doesn't surpass 40 degrees Celsius. When all is dry, pour into a Pyrex glass mortar and grind it into a fine powder. When you execute this operation, protect your mouth and nose with a mask, because this Martial salt, if it were breathed, provokes coughing.

Place the mortar containing the powder spread thin in sunlight for some days, until all the acrimony disappears, which you will recognise by the absence of the smell of vinegar.

Put this salt into a matrass and pour in spirit of wine at 100 percent purity, enough to dissolve the material. Digest as previously and then filter. Keep the tincture in a glass flask, very tightly closed and sheltered from the light.

This tincture of Mars (see Plate II-k) will be useful with all illness where a Martial influence is preferred.

Caution! All the metallic tinctures made by an expert Artist should only be given in homoeopathic doses, under the direction of a specialist.

TINCTURE OF GOLD
OR OF THE SUN

D issolve in a graduated glass flask (Becker) 25 millilitres of Aqua Regis (*Royal Water*) prepared with three parts of the spirit of salt and one part of spirit of nitre, and 2-3 grams of pure gold. To increase the speed of the dissolution, heat up the *Royal Water* to 40 degrees Celsius. After the dissolution is complete, pour into a 50 millilitre graduated glass test tube.

Pour into this water that contains the Sun in dissolution, with much caution, 25 millilitres of sulphuric ether.

After some time, you will see the ether tinctured a beautiful yellow colour. But, if that doesn't happen, introduce a glass rod into the liquid, into the bottom of the test tube, shake it once and remove it.

The gold in dissolution in the *Royal Water* passes into the ether. When you verify that the ether begins to react with the Royal Water, it is time for you to remove all the tinctured ether with a glass pipette, then pour it into a retort with a 250 millilitre bowl.

Place the retort into a sand bath on a small electric stove with controlled temperature. Distil with a very gentle heat all of the ether, until what remains is reduced to thick oil. At this time, remove the retort from the stove.

After cooling, pour into the retort 50 millilitres of spirit of wine at 100 percent purity, which will dissolve the oil quickly and it will be tinctured a beautiful yellow colour. Digest as in the previous operation and filter it through a glass funnel with a small cotton lid. Keep the tincture in a flask, tightly closed and sheltered from the light.

This magnificent Gold or Sun tincture (see Plate II-k) will be useful in all diseases where it is suitable to introduce a solar influence. It should be used in homoeopathic dosage.

Gentlemen living room alchemists that never stained yellow your delicate hands in the preparation of the Star King's solvent water and whom, in your speeches, philosophical, you imagine to know the passage of our Art, tend now to your opportunity to learn something of the works of these great Masters for your philosophical divagations.

Ora et labora

GLOSSARY OF WEIGHTS AND MEASURES

Although the author does not refer extensively to the following weights and measures in his little work, the editor remains convinced that their inclusion is warranted, and on the grounds that an understanding of such will greatly enhance the serious student of the Art's reading of the original, frequently instructional texts referred to throughout this book.

Grain
Weight measure corresponding to 0.0648 grams.

Gros
Measure of equivalent weight for 3.55 grams.

Lot
Old equivalent German weight measure for 14.17 grams.

Mark
Old weight measure for gold and silver corresponding to 16.6 grams.

Ounce
Old measure of equivalent weight for 28.349 grams.

Pound
Unit of equivalent mass for 453.59 grams (England).

Scruple
Old weight measure corresponding to 1.296 grams.

It should also be noted that the author uses the degrees Baume system of measuring the density of various liquids, and that some students of the Art may need to calculate conversions to suit the measurement systems common to their own country or operative practice. Further, the author's referral to glassware joint sizes is not to universal standards.

BIBLIOGRAPHY

Alchemie et medicine – Alexander Von Bernus, Paris, 1960.

An Open Entrance to the Closed Palace of the King – Eirenaeus Philalethes, An Anonymous Sage and Lover of Truth, 1702. See http://www.alchemywebsite.com/openentr.html

Azoth, ou Le moyen de faire l'or caché des Philosophes – Basil Valentine, Paris, 1659.

Chimie Moderne – M. AD. Wurtz, Professeur de Chimie de la Faculté de Médecine et La Faculté des Sciences de Paris, M DCCC LXXXIV.

Cours de Chymie – M. Lemery, de L'Académie Royale des Sciences, Docteur en Médecine, Paris, M DCC LVI.

Currus Triumphalis Antimonii or The Triumphal Chariot of Antimony, With the Commentary of Theodore Kerckringius, A Doctor of Medicine – Basil Valentine, Edmonds, WA: The Alchemical Press / Holmes Publishing Group, 1992. See http://www.alchemywebsite.com/antimony.html

Dictionaire Mytho-Hermétique – Dom Antoine Joseph Pernety, Religieux Bènèdictin de la Congrègation se Saint Maur, Paris M DCC LVII.

Douze Clefs or Twelve Keys, in The Last Will and Testament of Basil Valentine, Monke of the Order of St. Bennet – Basil Valentine, London, S.G. and B.G. for Edward Brewster, 1672, and later in Richardson, Texas, Restoration of Alchemical Manuscripts Society / R.A.M.S., 1978. See http://www.alchemywebsite.com/twelvkey.html

His Exposition of the Hieroglyphicall Figures which he caused to bee painted upon an Arch in St. Innocents Church-yard, in Paris – Nicholas Flamel, London, 1624.
See http://www.alchemywebsite.com/flam_h0.html

L'Alchimie Expliquee sur ses Textes Classiques – Eugene Canseliet, A. Paris Chez Jean-Jacques Pauvert, 1972.

Les Fondements de l'Alchimie de Newton – Betty J. Teeter Dobbs. Guy Trédaniel, la Éditions Maisnie, Paris.

Testament of Nicholas Flamel – Nocholas Flamel, London, Printed by J. and E. Hodson ... and sold only by the Editor, 1806.
See http://www.alchemywebsite.com/testment.html

The Last Will and Testament of Basil Valentine, Monke of the Order of St. Bennet – Basil Valentine, London, S.G. and B.G. for Edward Brewster, 1672, and later in Richardson, Texas, Restoration of Alchemical Manuscripts Society / R.A.M.S., 1978.

The Marrow of Alchemy – Eirenaeus Philalethes, Codex Press, 1990.

The Summary of Philosophy – Nicholas Flamel.
See http://www.alchemywebsite.com/flamsumm.html

Théories & Symboles des Alchimistes, Le Grand Œuvre – Albert Poisson, Éditions Traditioneles, Paris V., 1981, Reproduction de l'édition de 1891.

Traité De La Chymie – Christophle Glaser, Apotiquaire Ordinaire du Roy et de Monseigneur le Duc de Orleans, Paris, M DC LXVII.